WRITING for the Web

WRITING for the
Web

Crawford Kilian

Self-Counsel Press
(a division of)
International Self-Counsel Press Ltd.
USA   Canada

*Self-Counsel Press acknowledges the financial support of the Government of Canada
through the Book Publishing Industry Development Program (BPIDP) for our publishing activities.*

Printed in Canada.

First edition: 1999; Reprinted: 2000
Second edition: 2000
Third edition: 2007
Fourth edition: 2009

Library and Archives Canada Cataloguing in Publication

Kilian, Crawford, 1941-
    Writing for the web 3.0 / Crawford Kilian. — 4th ed.

    ISBN 978-1-55180-831-4

Permissions
The author gratefully acknowledges that the following have generously given
permission to reproduce their materials, in whole or in part, in this book:

    In Chapter 5, reference to materials in *Prioritizing Web Usability* (Berkeley:
New Riders, 2006), by Jakob Nielsen and Hoa Loranger.

    In Chapter 6, personal quotations from correspondence with Marijke Rijs-
berman and Stephen Martin.

    1. World Wide Web. 2. English language — Rhetoric — Data processing.
3. Web sites--Design. Title.
TK5105 .888.K365 2009   808'.066005   C2009-900693-6

Self-Counsel Press
(a division of)
International Self-Counsel Press Ltd.

1704 North State Street	1481 Charlotte Road
Bellingham, WA 98225	North Vancouver, BC V7J 1H1
USA	Canada

CONTENTS

This book is dedicated to all those friends and colleagues who participated in creating it, and to everyone who helps to create the Web by writing for it.

NOTICE TO READERS

PREFACE

For over 40 years I taught workplace writing, freelance article writing, and how to write commercial fiction. This is my 20th book. So I'm pretty dedicated to print on paper as a medium of communication.

But in the late 1980s I began to see how networked computers were changing the way we communicate. In some ways they were just another means of getting print on paper. But something about the medium itself was changing the nature of our messages — and changing our relationships with the people we communicated with. First in email, and then on the newfangled World Wide Web, we were reading, writing, and reacting to information in different ways.

In teaching technology students in the early 1990s, I had to learn fast to stay ahead of them. We were all scrambling to master the new grammar of multimedia: the ways that text and sound and image could combine to express ideas. With few authorities to consult, my students and I watched what we ourselves were doing, and we tried to draw general principles from our experience.

By the mid-1990s the Web was truly worldwide, and a whole new industry arose to serve and advance it. I got a sense of how big it was when I walked into a university bookstore and found, by rough estimate, 170 shelf-feet of books about the Web: how to master HTML, CGI, and Java; how to use this or that browser; how to design websites; how to research the exponentially growing resources available on the Web.

Not one of those books dealt with the actual words to be used on the Web.

Well, that made a certain amount of sense. No one had enough experience yet to say what would work on the Web, and what wouldn't. Hypertext had been around in various forms since the 1970s, but it wouldn't necessarily work on the Web the way it does, for example, on an encyclopedia DVD.

So most of the Web pioneers wrote in whatever style seemed comfortable, and other pioneers followed their lead. That's why, in the late 1990s, so many sites had expressions like "Check it out" and "This site under construction."

By then, creating websites had changed from a self-taught skill into an industry. The pioneers had given countless hours to trial and error (mostly error), in learning the basics of a new technology. But they couldn't squander their time when clients were paying for it. An obscure computer specialty in 1992 had, by the end of the decade, become almost a basic job skill. My own colleagues, teaching in fields like tourism and business administration, began to wonder how they could cram website design into an already crowded curriculum.

So the time seemed right for a book that might help both expert and novice webwriters save time and avoid known pitfalls. It might thereby help Web users as well.

This book doubtless reflects my own biases toward print on paper, but I have tried to learn from a wide range of self-taught pioneer Web authorities and to present their views as well as my own. If my arguments make sense and help you write successful text for your sites, of course I'll be delighted. But I look forward to being rebutted and superseded, because better insights will make webwriting a more effective communication tool for all of us. Some of my arguments may provoke you into articulating contrary views that help to make your sites succeed. If so, this book has succeeded too.

In mastering webwriting, we learn about what goes on in other kinds of writing as well, and what goes on in our own minds. So in learning to write well for this medium, I think we learn how to write better in all media, and we learn something about ourselves as well.

ACKNOWLEDGMENTS

As I look back on this book through four editions, I can see it's been created very interactively. Many people responded to earlier editions or excerpts, making me reconsider my earlier views.

I thank the online colleagues who graciously permitted me to quote from their email correspondence, websites, and published books: Robert E. Horn, Stephen Martin, Jakob Nielsen, Debbie Ridpath Ohi, Gareth Rees, and Marijke Rijsberman. A special thank-you to Steve Outing and Amy Gahran, whose Online Writers mail list, and late lamented Content Exchange website, provided lively forums for discussion of this new medium.

My own students in Canada and Brazil have contributed greatly to my understanding of online writing. I should thank those in particular who prodded me to make myself clearer as I taught (and learned) the principles of hypertext writing: Bev Chiu, Besire Culhaoglu, Luis Filidis, Kelly Gomes, David Ingram, Raj Kamal,

Sarah King, Rhona MacInnes, Adrian McInnes, Ross McKerlich, Sandy Meyer, Michelle Morelos, Deirdre Radomske, Mercedes Sanchez, Gabriela Schonbach, and Michael Souvage.

Special thanks as well Dr. Dennis Jerz and his students at Seton Hill University: The students' blogged responses to the third edition gave me very useful feedback. I hope it's reflected in much of this edition's new content.

I also thank Judy Phillips, who edited the first edition of *Writing for the Web*; Richard Day, who edited the second; Barbara Kuhne, who edited the third; and Eileen Velthuis, who edited this fourth version.

INTRODUCTION

Twenty years after Tim Berners-Lee wrote his first proposal for "a large hypertext database with typed links," most of us don't know how we ever got along without the World Wide Web. Yet old habits die hard, and we still use the Web with habits acquired in other media.

So newspaper websites still look a lot like newspapers. TV station websites offer lots of video. Business websites look like their ads in the Yellow Pages, only with more colors. And most website creators treat it like whatever medium they're most familiar with: a sheet of typing paper, a radio, a canvas, a family photo album, or a Rolodex.

Websites can serve all those functions, but one of their primary purposes is to make large amounts of text available online. (The Latin word for "web," by the way, is *textus*.) Graphics and sound can enhance the content of a site, but text remains the core.

The Web is a very different medium from print, TV, and radio. But the habits we've learned in those media influence the way we respond to text on the computer screen. We even call web files "pages" when they're nothing of the sort.

We read print documents in a certain way, using cues to navigate through a familiar format. The indented first line of a paragraph tells us a new topic is coming up. Page numbers establish a sequence we're happy to follow. Indexes use alphabetical order to help us find things. We're so used to these conventions that we don't even notice them.

But print habits don't apply on the Web. We surf through TV channels with our remote control, and we bring the same attitude to the TV-like screen of our computer: deliver something interesting right now, some kind of jolt or reward, or we'll go somewhere else.

These responses demand a kind of writing that is different from other media — not better or worse, just different. Effective website creation can certainly include excellent video, graphics, and sound. But it also means text that can interest impatient surfers and make them read what you've written.

This book offers some principles for composing text for your website. The principles aren't carved in stone (how could they be?), but they arise from the experience of thousands of people writing online and on the Web over the past 20 years. We can draw some general conclusions from that experience: what works and what doesn't. We can also modify or ignore those conclusions if our own circumstances require us to. When George Orwell compiled his list of rules for clear writing, he saved the best for last: "Break any of these rules sooner than say anything outright barbarous." Good webtext has a lot in common with good print text. It's plain, concise, concrete, and "transparent": Even on a personal website, the text should draw attention to its subject, not to itself. This book will give you plenty of exercises and tips for developing such a writing style.

Like good print text, webtext carries a subtext, a nonverbal message. The message may be, "I'm comfortable in this medium and I understand you, my reader." Or it may be, "I'm completely wrapped up in my own ego and my love of cool stuff." This book should help to sensitize you to any writing habits that may let the wrong subtext slip out.

I can't tell you how to design your site. But I can try to alert you to the likely results of your design decisions. For example, if you like long, long paragraphs full of long, long words, your readers will soon lose interest in what you have to say.

Similarly, if your text scrolls on forever, you will lose readers. If you build your site with layer after layer of linked pages, you will likely baffle and bore your readers.

If you are creating your own commercial site, or a personal blog, you decided the content and the structure: its topics, its size, how its pages connect, how its graphics, text, audio and video work together. For reasons I'll discuss, you can easily undercut yourself by presenting text as if it were still on paper. So it's in your own interest to understand something about website design basics, especially as they affect the display of your text.

You face other constraints, if you're writing text for a site designed by someone else. The site designer may not have known or cared about the kind of text displays you need. Navigation aids may not be good enough. All too often, such sites are designed by techies who go with what looks cool, not with what users need. Or a senior manager with no knowledge of the Web may have the final word on both design and content.

How to write good text is only one of your challenges if you're working on a corporate website. You may need to explain some basics about the medium to your colleagues — and again, while I don't deal directly with design issues, you'll need to understand some realities about the medium if you're going to use it effectively. And whether you're writing for a small personal blog or a big corporate website, effectiveness is the whole point of your effort.

❯❯❯

So let's start at the beginning, with what makes your computer screen a different medium from the printed page you're reading right now.

Print text relies on what is technically called "hypotaxis": one idea clearly linked to the last idea, and linked in turn to the next idea. Words like "therefore," "nevertheless," "third," "moreover," "similarly," and "so" are the links in hypotactic text. Most of us are very comfortable with this kind of patient construction.

Hypertext relies on "parataxis," ideas that stand alone without such links. This can be confusing, but if your readers can make the connections by themselves, the impact of your text is enormous. Go out on a first date and hear a good band play a good song. Marry your date, and every time you hear that song, parataxis will take you back to the night your life changed forever.

When they're playing your song, you feel a jolt as you connect with that special night. When your computer links you to something that really matters to you, you experience a similar jolt.

Computers condition us for "high joltage." A jolt is an emotional reward that follows a prescribed action. Turn on the TV at the right time for your favorite program, and it delivers jolts. Watch a movie, and it delivers jolts. Log on to your favorite forum or chat room, and you get jolts of praise or blame.

Like Pavlov's dogs, computer users are now conditioned to expect such stimuli. Maybe it's a jolt of surprise as our computer beeps or boings. Maybe it's a jolt of triumph as we find information we've been looking for. Or a jolt of satisfaction when someone has linked to our blog because we've posted something good.

Yes, it's a kind of addiction. We feel deprived if we don't get some kind of jolt at regular intervals, so we go where we hope to find more jolts — to websites.

Does this mean your own site needs to look and sound like a rock video? Or that you need to use obscene language to get and keep your visitors' attention? Not at all.

A truly high-joltage website supplies the information its visitors are looking for. But your text had better be invitingly concise, and it should provide the simple jolt of being understandable in one quick glance.

If it also intrigues your visitors by offering them a hook of some kind so they'll keep reading, so much the better. Your role as a webwriter is to make your reader's job effortless.

To sum up: By combining text, graphics, video, and audio, the Web offers some of the qualities of familiar media like print, TV, movies, and radio. When we recognize these qualities, we respond as if we were dealing with those media. As a writer, you should understand your visitors' mindset and compose your text accordingly.

You should also understand and accept the strengths and weaknesses of the Web. Your readers may want to treat your site like a book or magazine or TV show, but it's still a website — a collection of electronic files that you can organize as you please, but that your visitors will explore as they please.

That puts you in an interesting bind: You may think of it as text, but it's really hypertext — a paratactic mess of words and ideas that your readers will put together in a way that may or may not make sense to them. In Chapter 1, we'll look at what that means for you as a webwriter.

This fourth edition of *Writing for the Web* is also a kind of hypertext. You can access an electronic supplement through my blog Writing for the Web (http://crofsblogs.typepad.com). The supplement has a PowerPoint slide show, links to sources mentioned in the book, and continuous updates.

I will also add whatever new materials I find that might be useful, and materials that you let me know about. This is, after all, an interactive medium.

❯ ❯ ❯

1

HISTORY, HYPERTEXT, AND INTERACTIVE COMMUNICATION

As World War II was nearing its end, an American scientist named Vannevar Bush published an article, "As We May Think," (http://www.theatlantic.com/doc/194507/bush).

As director of the wartime Office of Scientific Research and Development, Bush understood very well that information had become almost unmanageable. The atomic bomb was a top-secret project fully known to only a few hundred scientists. Yet even the bomb had generated a whitewater flood of information. Government, business, science — every field was generating so much information that no one could follow it.

Computers in Bush's day were huge and crude, but microfilm was beginning to put whole bookshelves' worth of information onto small reels of celluloid. A little electric motor could zip you through weeks' worth of newspaper pages, or the pages of a long technical report — all projected onto a small screen. Bush dreamed of a camera that would take pictures of the pages you wanted to, so you could revisit them whenever you liked.

Microfilm never fulfilled Bush's dreams, but as recently as the 1970s, the microfiche looked like a serious step forward: a hundred pages of text on a sheet of film the size of a postcard!

As a young technical writer in the mid-1960s, I saw the scientists at the Lawrence Berkeley Laboratory struggling to keep up with "the literature" — the articles published in their narrow specialties. Computers by then were less crude, but they could still fill a large room. Some of the lab's tech writers were using them to help scientists refine their searches, but it was a slow and painful process. The tech writers didn't know it, but they were trying to create Google.

At almost exactly the same time, a young computer genius named Ted Nelson launched the Xanadu Project (www.xanadu.com), an attempt to realize Vannevar Bush's dream using something Nelson called "hypertext." It wasn't (and isn't) what we now called hypertext. On the home page of the Xanadu Project, the World Wide Web is dismissed as "another imitation of paper [that] trivializes our original hypertext model." Perhaps it does. But the Web is what we're now stuck with, and "hypertext" is the term we use to describe how we use the Web: a way of connecting text, graphics, video, and audio that uses computers to realize the dream of Vannevar Bush.

Is it Web or web?

 Technically, the World Wide Web is a proper noun, usually shortened to Web. But the weight of usage in the last few years has been to use lower case except when referring to the Web as a system of linked sites and pages. So in this book I'll use lower-case w (webwriting, website) except when referring to the Web itself.

---

1. Plain Text versus Hypertext

If you want to learn about, say, vampires, you face a pretty tedious process if you plan to research the topic using a multi-volume encyclopedia. First you would go to the volume with all the V entries, and find "Vampires." That entry may suggest you also look at entries in other volumes: Transylvania; Dracula; Stoker, Bram; Lugosi, Bela; films, horror; bats, vampire; films, German: Nosferatu. As you consult each of these entries, you're pulling heavy volumes off the shelf and replacing them, making notes, and generally taking up a lot of time.

Even using a single-volume book to research a topic presents challenges. Such a book may have its own hypertext in the form of footnotes, endnotes, appendixes, bibliographies, and an index — even marginal scribbles by the last reader. The researcher looking for particular information soon learns to read backward: Start with the index and then jump to just the pages dealing with the subject of interest. Even then, the follow-up of tracking down footnoted references and finding titles mentioned in the bibliography can be tedious and frustrating.

Hypertext saves you much of that work. Each hypertext document has electronic links to other hypertext documents, much like doors between rooms in a library. If you're reading a hypertext document about vampires (http://en.wikipedia.org/wiki/Vampire) and you find a mention of Bela Lugosi, the actor's name can itself be a link to still more information. Instead of making notes, you can simply save the file about Lugosi along with all the other items you've encountered.

And if you don't want to read about Bela Lugosi, but you do want to read about vampire bats or Transylvanian history, you can ignore the link to the Hollywood star and continue your reading.

This freedom of choice has its attractions, but some hypertext pioneers have tried to make it look like a revolution on a Gutenbergian scale. They claim that, freed from the tyranny of the author's structure, readers can now examine any document they like, in any order they choose, and use the information any way they please. (Of course, readers can also read a print document any way they please, but it takes more effort to jump back and forth in a print-on-paper document than in an electronic document.)

If each item of information is small enough, maybe just a paragraph or even a sentence, then readers have even more freedom. Instead of being led like children by the author's hand, readers can now make the text their own property, linking its components in their own preferred way.

This freedom of choice also has its limits. If we just want to find out about Bram Stoker, we don't want to waste time on Bela Lugosi, even if the author thinks Lugosi is important.

But most of the time, as readers, we expect the author to have mapped out our route for us, just as we expect a travel agent to plan details of our trip. We assume the travel agent knows more than we do and can anticipate our needs. Maybe we want some flexibility built into our itinerary, but we don't want to fly from New York to Paris, back to New York, and then to Frankfurt.

Pushed to a logical extreme, the hypertext author might as well hand the reader a set of Scrabble tiles and say: "Here, make your own text." But that's not authorship, any more than 52 Pickup is a card game. Our readers expect some kind of coherence in our hypertext. We can and should provide such coherence, but we should be aware of some specific challenges in doing so.

Hypertext is by definition nonlinear, but remember that "linearity" itself is just a metaphor for a one-at-a-time sequence — especially a sequence we're familiar with. The sequence A-B-C is "linear" only because that's the sequence we have learned. So is 1-2-3, and so is subject-verb-object. Because we've memorized certain patterns, we can expect D to follow C, 3 to follow 2, and verb (usually) to follow subject.

When we put information into a numbered sequence, for example, we expect #1 to be more important or more basic than #2. That's because we're used to hearing important or introductory material before we hear details or complicated material that assumes we understand the basics.

What is hypertext, anyway?

An essay or paper with footnotes or a bibliography is a kind of hypertext since it refers to other documents in a way that makes it fairly easy to find them. A document with marginal annotations could also be called a hypertext. But in this book, "hypertext" refers to linked documents in electronic format (files on a hard drive, a CD, or a DVD containing text, graphics, audio, video, or some combination of these elements). The link enables readers to jump between documents — even if the documents are on remote computers far away from one another.

---

2. The Interactive Communication Model

In the rest of this book, I'll examine some of the problems — and opportunities — that hypertext offers to you as a webwriter. But you should also bear in mind that hypertext depends on a completely different kind of communication model from print, film, TV and radio: the online medium is interactive, and that makes a huge difference in what you say and the way you say it. It even creates a different culture from that of earlier media.

The standard model, also called the instrumentalist model, treats a message like a FedEx package. All the recipient has to do is sign for it: buy the product, vote for the candidate, give the right answer on the exam, keep to the speed limit. The message is the instrument that makes the recipient behave in some desired way.

In the interactive model (also called the constructivist model), both sides are creating a conversation. They are construing the meaning of that conversation by learning more about each other.

The unspoken message in the standard model is "Do what I say." In the interactive model, the unspoken message is "Is this what you want?" As we will see, many corporate websites (both business and government) still operate on the standard model. Their sponsors see your computer screen as just another spot where they can slap up a copy of their one-way message.

Good webwriting, though, should exploit this opportunity for a two-way conversation — whatever the purpose and content of your site.

As I've watched the interactive culture emerge online since the 1980s, I've seen its key traits emerge. The standard culture wants to know the right answers; interactive culture wants to know the right questions. Standard culture likes to learn from success; interactive culture learns more from failures and mistakes. Standard culture looks to the future; interactive culture is impatient, demanding just-in-time results.

Interactives tend to be egalitarian, respecting other people not for their social status or rank, but for their expertise and willingness to share it. Standard culture waits for someone to give the order; interactives decide what to do and then do it.

I'm not suggesting that interactive culture is somehow better than that of the standard model — it's just different, and it's different because of the technology that the interactive model emerges from. That technology gives you, as a webwriter, both limits and opportunities. As you develop content for your website, you should bear in mind some basic facts about the medium and its users.

3. Computers Make Us Impatient

We used to call it the World Wide Wait, because the primitive dial-up systems of the 1990s were so slow to load pages. Many users in those days would set their browsers to ignore the graphics; always the slowest items to load.

That impatience is still with us. But now we're impatient to get right to the material we came looking for, and we're likely to hit the Back button if we can't find it right this instant.

4. Computers Give Us Jolts

When you're driving a car or riding a bike, it gives you instant feedback on your actions. Ideally, so do computers. Click on an icon and you get music, or a window opens, or email pops up. Text itself can give us jolts — anything from seeing our name on someone else's site, to reading a message from an old friend, to finding a scrap of information we've been searching for.

A "high-joltage" website will attract and hold more visitors than one providing little stimulus. This doesn't mean writing in a hysterical style; it means writing clear text with your readers in mind.

5. Computer-Screen Text Is Hard to Read

You may not realize it but your monitor has awful resolution. Maybe the text looks crisp and sharp compared to that on those old green-on-black monitors of the mid-1980s. But take a look at your text onscreen and then at a laser printout. Once you look back at your screen, the printout will be a sight for sore eyes, and you'll realize how difficult it is to read lots of text onscreen.

Studies in the 1980s, reported by Web analyst and usability advocate Jakob Nielsen, found that reading from a monitor is 25 percent slower than reading print on paper.

This seems to result from the poor resolution of computer screens, and in 1998, Nielsen was reporting that expensive experimental monitors with very high resolution can bring reading speeds back up to normal. Modern computers do have higher resolution, but not everyone has a modern computer. For the foreseeable future, we should assume that screen text will be harder to read than print text.

So we're stuck trying to read text on low-resolution screens. We don't always consciously realize it, but reading 75 words of text on a computer monitor feels as long as reading 100 words on paper. For impatient, jolt-hungry readers, this is a problem.

Reading from a monitor is tiring in other ways as well: Try reading this book while holding it straight out in front of you at arm's length. When your arms get tired, just prop it up at the same distance. It feels unnatural because it is unnatural. You'd rather hold the book in your lap, or on a tabletop within a foot of your eyes.

To improve the readability of your text, you can provide lots of blank space around it, as you would in a résumé. This means limiting the amount of text you put on a single screen.

You may choose to display your text in a column that reaches only halfway across the screen, leaving wide margins on either side or areas of blank space that provide respite for your readers' eyes. While this display may mean that onscreen readers will have to scroll down the page to read the full article, shortening the length of the lines makes text more readable. This is why newspapers display text in narrow columns.

5.1 Computer-screen text is hard to proofread

Jakob Nielsen and others have found that the longer we read text on a screen, the worse our ability to spot mistakes. All kinds of errors and typos escape correction — especially in boldface headings and subheads. Our visitors, however, are likely to spot our mistakes very quickly.

6. Websites Attract Different Kinds of Visitors

Viewers and listeners are looking for graphics and sound. Text doesn't really interest them except as a guide to the next video clip, graphic image, or song. Listeners may also include persons with visual impairments who need text that's understandable when spoken by a voice program.

Users are looking for information. They include customers as well as researchers. They like "chunks" — stand-alone blocks of information, filling the screen with 100 words or less, requiring little or no scrolling. Users need concise, well-organized, and well-mapped sites so they can go straight to what they want.

Readers want information too, but they are willing to scroll through complete documents. They may well prefer text adapted for screen display. Better yet, they like printer-friendly versions that they can print out and read on paper.

Talkers are visitors who want to comment on what they find on your site, and perhaps create a link to it on their own sites — especially if they're running web logs (blogs) dealing with the same subjects you also deal with. (Thanks to my Brazilian student Luis Filidis for this insight.)

Colleagues may obtain your information through an intranet accessible only to employees. Such visitors need clear, usable, well-formatted information just as much as outsiders do.

Customers want to buy something from you. They certainly want information, but they also want clear, simple steps that let them buy what they want.

Depending on the nature of your site, you should try to appeal to as many different kinds of visitors as possible. If you're a graphic designer looking for work, for example, your site should feature many examples of your work — and also plenty of text describing your background, skills, and philosophy.

Bear in mind also that your visitors may not be native speakers of your language, or very highly educated. Your text needs to be understandable and usable to them as well.

7. Webtext Is Hypertext

Your visitors can jump around from one page to another in any sequence they like. This means that the content of every page should be able to stand on its own, without reference to other documents except through clear links. As a webwriter you should be able to create such stand-alone documents, and to make it easy for your visitors to jump to other documents on your site (or on other sites).

Given the nature of this medium, and the interactive, international culture it has encouraged, writing for the Web is often very different from writing for print on paper. But it is a skill well worth mastering.

2

STRUCTURING YOUR WEBSITE

As a web author, you should be mentally organizing your material into hypertext. Maybe your readers won't choose to follow your organization, but if you visualize some kind of pattern for your material, it will at least make your own writing easier. If you understand the built-in problems of navigation and reader behavior, you can minimize their effects. Throwing information into your website at random because you know that "hypertext is nonlinear" will only make your website chaotic.

Hypertext can be any length, from a single letter or numeral to the collected works of Tolstoy. But for ease of reading, a computer monitor should normally display the equivalent of only a third to a half of a page of double-spaced typescript — say about 100 words.

You can, of course, pack much more than that into a single screen, but only if you reduce the point size of your type to illegibility and single-space the text. This is sure to drive your readers away; the eye recoils from unbroken masses of text, whether on a page or a screen.

You have just two choices for organizing your material: chunk it or scroll it. How you organize your material depends on the material itself and the uses your readers are likely to make of it. The Web is good for two kinds of information retrieval: hit and run, and downloading.

1. Chunking: Hit and Run Information Retrieval

Hit and run information retrieval is what most of us do when we surf the Web. We visit a site, see if anything looks interesting, click on it, get our jolt (or fail to get it), and go on to another site. Maybe we found nothing much or maybe the site changed our lives, but the information we retrieved was probably contained on one screen. The author had to present it as briefly and dramatically as possible so we would be interested in and understand it, and perhaps go on to other small chunks of information within the site. (Many webwriters use the word "chunk" to describe whatever information you can fit on a single screen; we'll use the term in this way also.)

When chunking, you break your material up into segments of not much more than 100 words (often much less), so that every word within a chunk is visible on a monitor screen. This pattern helps the reader to grasp all the information on the page. Two or more chunks, when linked electronically, form a "stack." Links will take readers to other pages in the stack, often by several different pathways.

A chunk may include more than one paragraph, and may also include headings, subheads, and graphics — even links to video and audio. It often helps to display chunked text double-spaced for easier reading.

However, some visitors are reluctant to explore the next page in the hypertext stack. You'd better make sure your first page provides plenty of reasons for readers to explore deeper into your stack. I'll discuss ways to do so in the next chapter. I'll also discuss ways to organize chunked text into clear hierarchies.

Sound and pictures can undercut text

In the early days of television commercials, advertisers discovered to their horror that they were sabotaging themselves by using images so fantastic that viewers were distracted from the products being advertised. They already knew that viewers wanted jolts in the form of vivid and dramatic images, even if they were in black and white. However, only with huge budgets could advertisers afford to feed that appetite.

What's more, advertisers felt they had to outdo their competitors, who were also trying to stop viewers from heading for the bathroom during the commercial breaks. So advertising was filled with wild and wonderful images that would command attention.

But when advertisers did follow-up interviews and market research, they learned that consumers rarely connected the fantastic images on the screen with the products that the images were supposed to help sell. The images were actually making people tune out the message.

Rosser Reeves, a 1950s advertising guru, called this effect "vampire video." Once he'd understood and named the problem, his commercials didn't abandon graphics, but the images became strictly subordinate to the message. Sometimes they were even the message itself: if viewers turned off the sound, they still got the sales pitch delivered as onscreen text.

Reeves's ads passed the critical test: people got the message and bought the product.

The Web is now in a stage comparable to 1950s television advertising and 1980s computer design. Remember when computers began to offer simple graphics and a choice of fonts? Remember the cluttered documents people produced, with several fonts per page, plus Dingbats and clipart as far as the eye could see? Website creators are doing awful things with graphics and audio, partly because they can and partly because they don't yet know they shouldn't.

Your choices as a web author will depend on the relative importance of text and graphics on your website. If you're a graphic artist displaying your work, your text will be minimal, even nonexistent.

If text is critical, then bells and whistles should appear only when they enhance the message (that is, if they make it more understandable, more surprising, more persuasive, or make reading it easier and more interesting).

2. Scrolling: Information Retrieval by Downloading

Sometimes readers surf for very detailed information online — perhaps a government report or a long news story, or maybe even a whole book. It would be pointless to break up such texts into independent chunks to be read in any order; the original authors intended them to be read in a certain sequence, with all the usual navigation cues of linear text printed on paper. However, the text may be too long to fit on the screen all at once, so the reader must scroll through such documents.

Long, linear-text documents really belong back on paper, however, and your website is just an archive for them. You don't need to worry quite as much about brevity with these documents; readers who want to scrutinize them and not just scan them can download them to their hard drives and then print them out in whatever format they prefer.

However, many visitors to your website will read at least part of such an archive on the monitor, whatever the cost in slowed reading speed and eyestrain. This is often true of PDF files. Scrolling tires out most readers very quickly, so if you choose to use it, provide internal links, such as a list of keyword links at the top of the file. (If you have Adobe Acrobat, you can create internal links when you create a PDF document — and you can also create links in the PDF to other online documents.)

Clicking on an internal link will take readers directly to the section of interest, enabling them to rappel like rock climbers down the text. When they're through reading a particular section, they can jump back to the top to find something else. A list of keywords also provides a useful overview of the text's main parts. For details on navigation, see Chapter 3.

Displaying long text on a blog

 On many blogs, the author simply displays long posts as scrolling text on the site's front page. This creates an additional problem: If the blog displays just one long scrolling text, readers may not want to scroll down to see what else is on the page.

One solution, available through programs like TypePad, is to break the long post in two: a headline plus a few lines on the front page, with a link to a new page where the whole text is available. This allows visitors to go through the whole text if they wish, but they can also scan the front page for other posts and links.

You can also make reading long posts easier with a few simple adjustments to the layout of the text. If you display your text in a column about one-half to one-third the width of your screen, each line will be only about 10 or 12 words long. Most people find this to be a comfortable line length to read, although, of course, it means still more scrolling.

If you save an archived text as a PDF, of course you keep the format of the original document. That could be ordinary single- or double-spaced word-processed text, or it could be an elaborately designed report with color photos and other graphics. If you expect most visitors to download the archived text and print it out, then don't worry about its online readability.

If you do expect visitors to read your text online, probably as a word-processed file, you should single-space your documents, with a double space between paragraphs. That makes paragraph indentations unnecessary, and gives your readers a welcome patch of white space between paragraphs to make reading easier. Without such breaks, readers get lost in a mass of text.

When deciding whether to chunk or scroll your text, you're not facing a clear-cut decision between a "bad" design (long, scrolling text) and a "good" one (chunks of text): Both have their uses. As a writer, you must decide whether your material is more useful in chunks written for hit and run readers, or in scrolling text meant to be printed out on paper. Whether you're writing for the hit and run reader or the downloader, you should offer text that's as clear, brief, and useful as you can make it.

For a very different point of view on long webtext, see Amber Simmons's well-argued article "Reviving Anorexic Web Writing" (http://alistapart.com/articles/revivinganorexicwebwriting) in the online magazine *A List Apart*.

3. The Three Principles of Webtext

You may intend your website to be simply an electronic archive of writing designed for text on paper. Or you may be using hypertext in avant-garde literary experiments for small audiences. In such cases, you can happily ignore the advice that follows. Otherwise, whatever the purpose and content of your site, I suggest that your text should reflect three basic principles: Orientation, Information, and Action.

In a business letter, for example, you supply appropriate background information and standard formatting (Orientation) to help the reader make sense of your main message (Information) and to understand what should happen as a result of that information (Action). So you might explain that overcrowding in your warehouse is forcing you to offer widgets at unheard-of low prices, and customers can act on that information by calling your toll-free telephone number.

These principles operate very similarly in webtext.

3.1 Orientation: Where am I and how do I get around this site?

When visitors arrive at your site, they need two kinds of orientation: background knowledge about the site, and navigation aids to help them get around the site. So the home page of your site should orient your readers by telling them —

- what the site's about,

- how it's organized, and

- how to navigate it.

Sometimes the title of the site tells visitors what it's about:

Your Guide to Chesterton

Often, however, you may need a few lines of explanation (sometimes known as a subtitle or catchphrase):

The complete directory of Chesterton's tourist attractions, businesses, and municipal services.

You may also need to elaborate on your organizational principle:

This site consists of six main pages: Tourist Attractions, Lodging, Dining, Business Guide, Municipal Services, and Community News.

Or you may present those topics as a set of buttons or graphics. You may want to offer more direct links from the front page by making it look more like a table of contents:

Municipal Services

    City Hall

    Police

    Parks Department

    School Board

    Highways Office

    Hospital

I discuss navigation cues such as the table of contents and navigation buttons in more detail in Chapter 3.

In judging the effectiveness of your orientation, you can apply two secondary principles: Minimalism and Coherence.

3.1a Minimalism

Is the orientation you are supplying the least the reader needs? If you're tempted to begin an orienting statement with, "As you probably know," you can probably drop the statement altogether.

Minimalism also means you shouldn't put too many items on your site. Every item may potentially add to the reader's navigation problems, so be sure that each one has a good reason for being there. Sometimes a link to another site is all you need.

3.1b Coherence

Does a given chunk of text make sense on its own? If it deals with two or three ideas in 100 words or so, do you supply clear transitions from one idea to the next? Does this chunk behave like other chunks on your site?

For example, suppose you have a chunk describing a local hotel, with a link to nearby restaurants; will other "lodging" chunks also link in the same way to restaurants? Once your readers understand your navigation system, they will expect to use it throughout your site, so you should endeavor to be consistent.

Don't forget that since many readers may first come to your site through a page other than your front page, orientation is important on every single page of your website. But it need not always be quite as detailed as on your front page.

3.2 Information: The reason for the site's existence

Your site provides readers with information in the form of text and graphics, whether displayed on several linked pages or on one long, scrolling page. Whatever that information may include, two secondary principles are at work here: Clarity and Correctness.

3.2a Clarity

Your text should be understandable at first glance, even to readers with little formal education or from a different cultural background. If readers must puzzle over unfamiliar or ambiguous words, you are making them work harder than they need to.

This is true even if your site deals with a specialist topic. For example, maybe you've created a site about extensible markup language (XML), which is a way of writing code for websites that require highly technical information. Are you using long, complicated words just because you can, when shorter ones would really be more clear and straightforward? Even your expert readers deserve the simplest, clearest discussion you can provide.

3.2b Correctness

On one level, "correctness" means basics such as proper spelling, good grammar, and accurate names and addresses. This kind of correctness is also part of clarity because it helps readers understand your message more easily.

But every message has two components, verbal and nonverbal, and if they're in conflict, readers tend to trust the nonverbal "subtext" message. Spelling or grammatical errors on, say, a lawyer's website create a subtext about the lawyer's poor attention to detail. Any professional or business website must convey a subtext message of competence; errors in language basics and errors of fact under-cut that message.

3.3 Action: What people should do once they're informed

What action do you want your readers to take as a result of absorb-ing the information on your website? Should they email you, pro-vide a credit card number, subscribe to a newsletter, or click on the link to your advertisers? If you are going to get the results you want, you need to consider two secondary principles: A positive attitude and the "you" attitude.

3.3a A positive attitude

Even if your site is denouncing violations of human rights or the destruction of the environment, you must think your users can do something about those problems. Otherwise, why bother to create a site?

So when you present problems, suggested solutions should be close at hand: documents with important information, links to groups with political influence, or email addresses of powerful people.

A positive attitude is easier to express if you avoid negative expressions altogether. Consider the positive wording in the right-hand column below:

| You won't be disappointed | You're sure to be pleased |
| Please don't hesitate to email us | Please email us |

3.3b The "you" attitude

Webwriting should present facts and ideas in terms of the reader's advantage. So be sure to talk more about your reader than about yourself. Instead of writing:

I've listed the top 15 companies I consider a threat to the environment.

— you can write:

You can email your protests to the top 15 environmental polluters.

This is more than simple courtesy. Your readers have their own purposes for coming to your site, and you are there to serve those purposes. If you understand what your readers want and you anticipate their needs, your site will succeed and your readers will return.

Another hazard for the "you" attitude is "egophilia": the habit of starting sentences with expressions like "I feel" or "I think." You may do so, ironically, as a way of modestly reducing a flat assertion to a statement of opinion. But you're only injecting yourself into the sentence. Better to stick with the flat assertion.

Instead of writing —

I feel this is the best hiking trail in the park.

write:

This is the best hiking trail in the park.

Instead of writing —

I believe you'd be wise to take out travel insurance before you leave.

write:

You'd be wise to take out travel insurance before you leave.

Consideration is an important part of the subtext that conveys the "you" attitude. Your readers are doing you a favor by visiting your site, and you owe them a rewarding experience. Will they really want to scroll through your list of the 100 worst movies of all time? Will they follow one of your links to a File Not Found message? An out-of-date site with "link rot" (links that go nowhere) wastes readers' time.

So put yourself in your readers' shoes: If you were a stranger arriving at your own site, would you feel as if the site's creator had made a special effort to make life easy for you?

If we accept these three principles of webwriting — orientation, information, and action — several useful guidelines for structuring content emerge from them. The next chapter discusses them in detail.

3

ORGANIZING WEBSITE CONTENT

1. Orientation: Navigation Cues Provide a Site Overview

Robert E. Horn, in his book *Mapping Hypertext*, points out that linear text is full of cues that help the reader navigate. For example, organization of print text is hierarchical. We expect each section to include some general statement or thesis, supported by various kinds of evidence or illustration. We start a book with an overview or introduction that summarizes important points, and we often find that chapters of the book feature similar introductions.

In hypertext, says Horn, we need to present the whole hierarchy of the text in some kind of overview, such as a navigation bar with buttons that will take us to different sections within the text.

Your home page may include a big headline and a summary about the purpose of the site, but it should essentially be a table of contents. You can organize your hypertext in a number of ways, including —

- alphabetically,

- numerically,

- chronologically,

- graphically, or

- completely at random (which I don't recommend).

A list of employees' telephone numbers and email addresses would naturally be alphabetical — probably just a string of letter-links (A, B, C, etc.) across the screen. So would a list of departments within your organization. A sequence describing a process in time might be a numbered list; so might a categorical list of topics running from most important to least important.

Many websites use graphical contents pages. These can range from something as simple as an organizational chart to an elaborate map full of graphic cues: a cartoon of a policeman in a kiosk, for example, linking to the name and telephone number of the company's security officer.

Be careful when using graphical cues in the place of textual cues. Many new visitors may not recognize the cartoon as a link, which will defeat its purpose.

If you're confident that your graphics are intuitive and self-explanatory to anyone from any cultural or educational background, you don't have to worry about refining the text on your contents page. Otherwise, try to make your text as clear as possible, even if it seems redundant to those who do understand the graphics.

1.1 Understand how visitors scan web pages

In the last few years, research has explored just how we read online. In 2002, the Eyetrack III study observed over 40 people while they read online news sites. It found that they tended to start in the upper left-hand corner, moved from left to right, went to the bottom of the page, and then went back up the right-hand column.

Some of the Eyetrack findings were surprising. For example, larger type encouraged scanning; smaller type encouraged careful reading. Readers paid attention to blurbs if they were on the same line as the headline. Blurbs got more readers when they were short and the first two words grabbed attention. Readers paid attention to text first and photos second.

Other findings were predictable. Short paragraphs got twice the number of "eye fixations" as long paragraphs. And stories displayed in a single column (instead of two or three columns of text displayed across the screen) got more attentive reading.

Readers also liked summary descriptions introducing articles. These "decks" are longer than a regular blurb, but got 95 percent viewing even in boldface or italic typefaces — which are notoriously hard to read in long passages. What's more, people who read decks went on to read just as much of the article as when they read articles with no decks.

More recently, Jakob Nielsen conducted an eyetracking study on many different kinds of websites, not just news sources. He found an "F-shaped" reading pattern: Visitors would start at the top left, scan straight across, drop down, and scan to the right again. Then they'd scan the left side of the page, going straight down.

Nielsen concluded that users don't read text very thoroughly. The first two paragraphs must give the most important information (very much like a news story). Subheads, paragraphs, and bullets should start with information-carrying words.

The Eyetrack '07 report (http://eyetrack.poynter.org) found that online readers actually read more of a story than they would on paper — 77 percent versus 62 percent for readers of stories in broadsheet newspapers.

Eyetrack '07 also found two kinds of readers: methodical readers and scanners. Methodical readers start at the top and read to the bottom, and they use drop-down menus and navigation tools to find the stories they want. Meanwhile, scanners check headlines and other landmarks but not very much text until they find an interesting headline. But once they do find a good story, they read as much as methodical readers.

Short text, the study found, is not only attractive to online readers, but also helps them remember more facts from stories.

These findings tend to confirm an idea long known to business writers and tabloid journalists: We tend to pay most attention to text at the beginning and end of a sentence, and especially to text at the beginning and end of a paragraph.

If these "hot spots" carry strong information, they deliver a stronger jolt to the reader. Writers of bad-news letters use this principle when they bury the bad news ("we can't hire you"; "we're not compensating you") in the middle of a paragraph, with neutral information at the beginning and end.

The implications are clear. Long paragraphs have fewer hot spots, so on a website they deliver fewer jolts. They're also literally repulsive to many visitors, who recoil when they see a big block of text. Short paragraphs made of short sentences have more hot spots, and therefore more jolts. In general, hit and run readers will prefer the high-joltage sites.

1.2 Treat every page like a home page

A pop song of yesteryear might be the anthem of webwriters: "Shut the door, they're coming in the window."

Web surfers can directly access just about any page on your site that doesn't require a password. You can create a detailed, well-organized home page with a clear statement of your site's purpose and a good table of contents.

But if I ask a search engine to find pages that mention snowboarding, and one of your other pages features the word "snowboarding," I will go to that page without ever seeing the rest of your site, let alone your home page. I won't even know much about your site unless you give me information and navigation aids on your snowboarding page.

Every page on your site should at least have a link to your home page or display a table of contents. Then your readers who have entered your site "through the window" will at least know where they are and what else your site has to offer. The terms you use in the table of contents should be identical to the headings you have used in the text. Your readers want to find their way around your site with the least possible hassle. If each page has consistent, clear navigation guides, readers will be grateful.

Many sites now offer both a table of contents, and an index page that provides a direct link to each individual page on the site. An index page may not have room for blurbs, but it's a good idea to group pages into sections. So if your website on the town of Chesterton has a page for each hotel in Chesterton, list those pages in the index under a section on Lodging — not in alphabetical order by hotel name interspersed with all the other index entries.

1.3 Signal transitions with navigation buttons

In print text, paragraph indentations signal new topics or subtopics. Punctuation marks define relationships between words and phrases. And transition words and phrases (*e.g., meanwhile, secondly, nevertheless, a day later, another argument*), let readers know how each paragraph connects to the previous one. In hypertext, such transitions are generally meaningless because readers may jump from section to section in various sequences.

Linear text often prepares us for sequences:

Your journey through Mexico will include stays in Cuernavaca, Puebla, and Acapulco.

When we read sentences like this one, we expect descriptions of each Mexican city, in the order given. Hypertext can prepare us for such sequences only by some cue outside the sequence, such as navigation buttons labeled <u>Cuernavaca</u>, <u>Puebla</u>, and <u>Acapulco</u>.

Your home page may include not only links to different sections of your site but also links to different passages within a single page — especially if it's a long, scrolling page. This allows readers to skip up and down the page to the paragraphs they're most interested in.

Be careful about the directional terms you use to label your navigation buttons. Your readers aren't all arriving at your site via your front page. If Google brings your readers straight to your Puebla page, a navigation link that says <u>Back to Home Page</u> doesn't make much sense. How can they go back to some place they've never been? Why have a button that says Next if the page it links to has nothing to do with Puebla? It would be better to create navigation links that say <u>To Mexico Home Page</u> or <u>To Acapulco Page</u>.

If you are working with long, scrolling documents, provide ways to jump to the beginning and various sections of the document at the bottom of the page, and perhaps at intermediate stages:

<u>To Top of Financial Aid Page</u>

<u>To Chesterton College Policies Page</u>

<u>To Chesterton College Home Page</u>

Most websites today have a fairly standard layout: a banner giving the site's name, a string of links from left to right below the banner, and another string running down the left-hand side. Still, readers may find navigation a bit confusing until they've become familiar with your particular layout. You may do them a favor with some guidelines in a prominent spot: <u>Read Me First</u>, <u>Introduction</u>, <u>If You're New to This Site</u>, or some such cue.

2. Orientation: Headlines

Headlines can include the title of your site (the banner), the titles of individual pages, and subheadings that break up text. Like the thesis sentence of a paragraph, headlines tell readers what to expect, so they deserve some thought before you write them.

Ideally, the title of your site should tell readers what it's about: In Praise of Holly Cole, or Your Guide to Chesterton. Many of your readers will find you through a search engine that gives them the site title and the first few words of text. If your title is Paradise!, and your introductory text is "Here is the land the conquistadors sought," readers searching for Chesterton may not realize this is the site they've been looking for.

If you're skilled in HTML, you can write a meta-tag that some search engines will display instead of the first few words on your page. A keyword meta tag lists words and phrases that searchers might use; for example, *skiing, snowboarding, winter sports, hiking, alpine environment, recreation.*

Some sites load such keywords (invisibly) onto their home pages so that search engines will display the sites in the first batch of "hits" the engines turn up. Many search engines, however, will reject sites with lists of meta tags. If they find the word "skiing" repeated ten times in an invisible meta tag, the engines recognize that this is an attempt to get the site to the top of the list of hits, and will not display the site.

If you don't know how to create meta tags, don't worry. Just make sure the keywords that readers are likely to search for are in your title and first few lines of text. Search engines will usually include those lines in their lists of hits. If the first text on your site is just the titles of your navigation buttons — Home, News Releases, President's Message — readers won't have much sense of what's really on your site, so they may not take a chance on visiting it.

Keep your headlines close to the text they introduce. Usually, headlines, including subheads, should be just one double space from the first line of regular text that follows.

2.1 Use subheads

The Eyetrack III study found that subheads encouraged skimmers to stay with an online news story. That seems generally true for any kind of webtext. If you're writing and organizing your text in screen-sized chunks, subheads will prepare readers for the content that is to appear in the following chunk.

Since web readers tend to scan rather than read from line to line, each subhead is a kind of landmark. It tells readers what they will find in each section. Again, they save time by scanning for the subhead that they want.

You may even find that a single chunk of 100 words can still benefit from two or three subheads. A solid mass of 100 words, in 8 or 10 lines, does not invite reading. It needs at least a headline. The text should break into two or more paragraphs, with perhaps a subhead somewhere near the middle of the chunk.

The layout of subheads in webtext is much like that in print. Subheads tend to be boldface (or in color, or both), with white space above and text close below. In a two-line subhead, the second line should be shorter than the first.

If you've broken your text into chunks or clickable pages, every subhead ought to have at least five or six lines of body text following it before the end of the chunk or page.

If you're providing long, scrolling text, subheads will help to break it up into manageable lengths. If the document is over 1,000 words long, break it up with subheads, and create links to those subheads at the top of the page:

Financial Aid and Awards

General Information   Services of the Financial Aid Office

Scholastic Awards   Deadlines for Applications

Emergency Funding   Publications

Your readers now have the choice of scrolling through the whole section, or jumping to particular sections of interest.

2.2 Grab readers' interest: Hooks, links, and blurbs

For a word less than 100 years old, "blurb" has gone through some remarkable changes in meaning.

American humorist Gelett Burgess coined the term in 1907. He sketched a voluptuous blonde as cover art for a book jacket, and named her "Miss Blinda Blurb." For some time, sexy cover art was a blurb, but the word also came to mean any overdone praise of a book appearing on the jacket.

While that's still an accepted meaning, the pulp magazines of the 1920s and 1930s picked it up in a different sense — the brief sum-mary of a story appearing between the title and the text. (Print editors today more often use the word "deck" for this summary.) Its purpose was to tempt readers into investing the time to read the story.

On the Web, we now use "blurb" to mean a notice about what to expect on the other side of a link. Like the pulp magazines, we want our readers to make that jump and invest some time in our text. They're more likely to if they have a sense of what they're get-ting themselves into. Without that sense, they may be reluctant to wander into the labyrinth. In effect, we haven't given them ade-quate orientation for our site.

A good link should have two parts, though they may appear in a single word or phrase: a hook and a blurb. The hook — a term borrowed from magazine writing — is something at the beginning of a text that grabs reader attention. In our case, the hook is usually the text of the link itself: <u>Best Snowboarding in Colorado</u>, or <u>Typi-cal House Prices in Lynn Valley</u>. If you think that's enough to draw readers through the link, then fine. Bear in mind that you have a wide range of hooking devices to choose from:

- **Quotation Marks.** "We love to read text that someone is supposed to have actually spoken," said Crawford Kilian.

- **Question.** A question promises an answer, and we'll jump through the link to find it.

- **Unusual statement.** Anything surprising will give the reader a jolt and wonder what other bizarre things you may have to say.

- **Comparison/contrast.** Comparisons show how things are similar; contrasts show how they differ.

- **News peg.** A tie-in with some big current event can draw interest (but don't let the news peg go stale on you).

- **Promise of conflict.** An attack or refutation makes us want to read more.

- **Direct address.** Webwriting needs the "you" attitude, so talk right to the reader.

- **Rebuttal.** Disagreement means a fight, and we all love to watch.

These hooks may stand on their own, but sometimes you're trapped with text that may be confusing or ambiguous. When I taught in a Communications department, I got a lot of mail intended for our public-relations people (who worked in what was called "college relations"). What if you're trying to show the difference between your company's Information Systems department and your Information Services department? That's where a blurb comes in handy:

Information Systems

Computer support, webmaster, staff training.

Information Services

Public relations, technical editing, company newsletter, advertising purchases.

Even if your text link seems self-explanatory, a blurb may make it more inviting. Maybe your text link is <u>What makes a good business plan?</u> The implied promise of an answer becomes more explicit with a blurb like: "Six successful entrepreneurs offer practical advice."

Whatever hook you use, make sure it's appropriate. A promise of conflict, for example, had better deliver the conflict.

Subheads are especially helpful in selling. They can gain attention (Free!), spark interest (How to retire in two years!), and make readers act (Click here for your instant subscription).

You can also make life easier for your readers by turning both hook and blurb into links. Suppose you have a link to <u>Company Personnel Policies</u>. Make the jump and you find yourself on a page full of still more links. Give readers the chance to go directly to the policy they want:

<u>Company Personnel Policies</u>

Policies dealing with <u>Hiring</u>, <u>Probationary Period</u>, <u>Employee Evaluation Procedures</u>, <u>Health and Safety Issues</u>, <u>Conflict Resolution</u>, <u>Salary Scale</u>, etc.

If screen space permits, you can break the blurb into a bulleted list or columns; the point is still to guide readers where they want to go, as quickly and conveniently as possible.

Fight the urge to turn the blurb into a mini-essay of its own. The blurb should always be the least you can possibly do. If the word, phrase, or sentence enables readers to use the link confidently, it's done its job.

The blurb might also indicate whether the text on the other side is an archive (a text originally written for print on paper) or a chunk (a text of no more than 80 or 100 words designed for "hit and run" reading). Many news sites do this when they display a headline and the first paragraph of a story, with (<u>Full Story</u>) at the end. You might do this with your company's annual report, with a summary in chunk form and the blurbs <u>Full Text in PDF</u> and <u>Full Text in HTML</u> as links.

With a link to chunked text, the blurb can simply make the link more explicit (again guiding readers where they want to go):

<u>Student Tuition Fees</u>

Fees for the 2009 – 2010 academic year for <u>resident</u> and <u>international students</u>.

Whatever page your readers land on, they should have the opportunity to respond to what they find — and to you. An email link may seem self-evident, but it might get more traffic with a blurb:

crof@shaw.ca

I'd love to hear your opinion of this advice!

Exercise 1: Assessing Website Structure

Visit two or three corporate websites — your local college, a big-box retailer, a major trade union, a large charity — and judge for yourself how well they use headlines, subheads, blurbs, and links.

---

3. Information: Analyze Your Audience — and Yourself!

Are you looking for customers, converts, students, employers, kindred spirits? Are they experienced in using the Web, or complete novices? Do they speak English? Do they read it? To find out, you'll need both research and soul search.

In some cases, you can draw a detailed demographic analysis based on careful research: maybe you're trying to sell package tours to singles aged 18 to 34, or providing medical advice for parents of children with cystic fibrosis, or celebrating a pop singer who appeals to girls aged 13 to 17. Much of what you have to say — in both content and style — should reflect what you know about that readership.

In other cases, your subject will cross boundaries of age, gender, and nationality. Your audience will care about the research you've put into the subject, but it would be impossible to do similar research into the audience itself.

This is where research yields to soul search: you have to ask yourself what other fans of Holly Cole would really like to find on your site, or what information would excite potential applicants to your college's computer-animation program.

Whatever decisions you make about the nature of your desired audience, don't forget that many in that target group simply don't have access to the Web, or don't even know about your site. Meanwhile, many other people who are not among your desired audience may turn up out of curiosity or by accident. Presumably you want them to leave with a good impression of you, your organization, and your intended audience, even if they're not especially interested in the subject of your site. So even if your site is highly specialized, it should offer something to the casual visitor.

You should also think hard about your own reasons for creating or revising the site: Is it to make money, to attract tourists, to recruit supporters, to share an interest?

3.1 What's your exformation?

Let me explain "exformation" with an anecdote:

One day long ago, my grandfather and his friend Will Crawford, for whom I was named, went for a walk in the woods of rural New Jersey where they lived. On their return, my grandfather exclaimed to my grandmother, "We must have seen a million rabbits in the woods!" Uncle Bill, standing behind him, held up his hand, fingers outstretched, and silently mouthed the word: Five.

Ever since then, when someone in my family exaggerates, someone else will hold up a hand and repeat Uncle Bill's silent five.

But we don't have to repeat the whole story, because we all know it. Almost every family, every group, has some similar kind of communication — a running gag, a child's baby-talk name preserved as a nickname, a word used in a special way. People in the northern California village of Booneville even developed a local dialect, "Boontling," (http://en.wikipedia.org/wiki/Boontling)

back in the 1920s. After one young couple was caught in flagrante on a pile of burlap bags, the Boontling word for making love was "burlappin.'"

Now, terms like these, once understood, become extremely effective. They seem to pack an extra emotional punch. The smaller the cue, the more powerful the response. Five upheld fingers are a devastating retort to some long-winded claim.

But to get the impact, you don't send a lot of information — you send almost none. Instead you rely on the knowledge you know you share with your reader or listener.

Barack Obama understood this during the 2008 US presidential campaign. In one speech, after a debate, he described how his opponents had been trying to nail him with "gotcha" questions. Then he seemed to brush a little dust off his shoulders. The crowd roared — it was a reference to a 2003 rap video by Jay-Z (http://thetyee.ca/Mediacheck/2008/04/29/Cyberspace08). Obama's listeners knew the video, and he was telling them, very minimally, that he knew it too: He was part of their culture. (We older folks had to have it explained to us in ordinary news stories!)

A Danish writer, Tor Norretranders, invented a term for this in his book *The User Illusion*: "exformation." Exformation is short for "explicitly discarded information," the information you strip out of a message because you know your reader already has it. The more you share with your reader, the less you have to say.

Norretranders's prime example is a communication between the French novelist Victor Hugo and his publisher. On holiday just after the publication of his novel *Les Misérables*, Hugo sent the following telegram to his publisher: "?"

To which his publisher replied: "!"

The anecdote would of course lack all meaning, never mind emotional impact, if I hadn't supplied the background (the information).

For webwriters, exformation is a great big problem. How much of our text assumes shared knowledge? How much do we need to spell out? And is our exformation the same as our readers'?

Several years ago I gave a seminar on webwriting, using the second edition of this book as the text. Everyone in the group was a Canadian, except for one — a Brazilian who didn't understand the title of the first chapter, "Hype and Hypertext." What, she wanted to know, was "hype"?

Like a carefully explained joke, "hype" had lost most of its punch by the time I managed to translate the term.

Exformation was also a problem in the third edition of this book, which was a text in an American university's course on webwriting. The students had to blog about what they were reading; some complained that parts of their textbook were annoying because they already knew all that stuff. Of course, if I'd left those parts out of the book, other readers would have been baffled.

If exformation is a problem, it's also an opportunity. We always feel closer to those who share our exformation, and we trust them more. Remember that the Web is a medium that thrives on jolts. Strip all but the absolute minimum information out of your text, and your readers get a major jolt if they share your exformation.

But what if your readers come from all over the world, and from different generations? The knowledge you share with them is uncertain, but you know they're on your site looking for jolts, not long-winded explanations of one-liners. Explaining too much is almost as bad as explaining too little — it implies you think your visitors are ignorant.

Well, sometimes they are ignorant, and they do need to know the information that you've explicitly discarded. How to do it?

If your text is technical, or uses regional dialect, or has lots of unusual idioms, one solution is to create a glossary. Each unusual or difficult expression can be a link to its definition. Those sharing your exformation can skip the links; those who need the definition can make a quick hop and then hop back again.

Another approach is to provide "newbie" pages or links, clearly labeled on your home page, so that newcomers can master the basics while others deal with the subject on a more advanced level.

If your site is intended for those who read English as a foreign language, or who are trying to learn a technical vocabulary, you can simply add an explanation or definition in the text, or make it clear from the context. But what seems clear to you may be opaque to your readers, so it's wise to test your text before you put it before the world.

Exercise 2: Identifying Exformation

Visit Global Voices (http://globalvoicesonline.org), a blog aggregator that publishes posts from all over the world. Read some of the posts and make a brief note of terms, expressions, and allusions that you don't understand. Also note names you're not familiar with, whether of prominent persons or of locations. The bloggers assumed most of their readers knew those terms as part of their exformation.

Now Google those expressions and see what you can learn.

Try the same exercise with websites dealing with technical aspects of some profession you're not familiar with — for example, Marginal Revolution (http://www.marginalrevolution.com), about economics, or Real Climate (http://www.real climate.org), dealing with climate change. How well do the writers on such sites meet the needs of both colleagues and newcomers?

Write in Global English

 Only about one-third of Internet users are native English speakers — a much smaller proportion than in the 1990s. English is widely spoken as a second language, but non-native speakers have trouble understanding some kinds of usage.

Rachel McAlpine, a New Zealand webwriting expert, has published a book titled *Global English for Global Business*, and you can find the basics of Global English on her website at http:// www.webpagecontent.com/corp_archive/139/5/.

One of the great advantages of Global English is that it makes good webwriting for everyone. Short sentences with few fancy words make life easier for all readers of webtext.

For more on Global English, see Chapter 5 on editing webtext.

3.2 Create a "client brief"

In some cases, when you're creating the content for someone's site you need the most specific guidance you can get from your client. Even if you're writing text for your own personal site, your job will be easier if you have a clear idea of the image you want to convey. Here are some questions that a typical client brief might include:

1. **What are the short-term and long-term objectives of the site?** For example, do you want to promote immediate online sales to visitors who will become repeat customers?

2. **What are the demographics, values, attitudes, and lifestyles of your desired audience?** If you're aiming at under-30s, but your cultural references and values statements are all straight out of the 1960s, you're in trouble. (Take the Environics 3SC Survey at: http://3sc.environics.net/surveys/3sc/main/3sc.asp to get a sense of your own social values.)

3. **What personality traits should the site convey through its tone and manner?** A breezy style on a site for public-health professionals may drive away the visitors you want. But a personal blog should convey your own personality, whether breezy, angry, or meditative.

4. **What do your current visitors think of the site in its present form?** If you don't know, you'd better find out. A brief, easy-to-do survey could save you a lot of time and trouble.

5. **What is the general impression you want visitors to gain after they've spent some time on the site?** If you're a freelance accountant, you certainly want visitors to think you're highly skilled, very professional, and easily accessible.

6. **What kinds of content will foster a positive perception among visitors?** Maybe it's constant updates, or archives of hard-to-find historical data, or documents and forms that make it easy for visitors to do what they came for.

7. **About how much of your current site can be reused?** And do you need to revise or edit that old content? This question can force you to look at existing content much more critically, instead of shoveling it back in just because it's available.

8. **What are your desired start and completion dates?** These should be realistic but not too generous — a looming deadline can inspire more work than a far-off one.

9. **What activities would you like visitors to take part in on the site?** Join chats, put items in a shopping cart, take a quiz, download materials?

10. **What "gifts" can you offer visitors?** Web culture loves free stuff, so even a business site should give away something — if only a ticket for a 10 percent discount on your first purchase. Special-interest sites often form "rings" that enable visitors to jump to related sites. Such visitors clearly appreciate the service.

3.3 Organize consciously

Don't throw material onto your site at random, just because it's hypertext. You have several possible ways to organize your content.

3.3a Narrative order: What happens next?

Narrative order involves describing a process through time. If it's a fairly extended narrative ("My Six Months Backpacking Through Africa"), you might as well make it a single long document and treat it as a downloadable archive. If it's a short narrative, or breaks logically into subsections, it might work better in chunks.

For example, if you're describing the process of home brewing, each stage might get its own page. Readers can go to the page they're interested in without having to scroll through material they don't want. However, readers may want to print out the text explaining the whole process, so you could make it available as a single document elsewhere on your site. (Be sure to let readers know that it's available.)

3.3b Logical Order: Appeal to reason

When you present text in a logical order, you make an assertion, you bring in your documentation to back it up, and you come to a conclusion. This may get long-winded, so your arguments are likely to end up at archive length rather than in short, powerful chunks.

If you're really familiar with the Web, you may be tempted to simply mention your sources and turn them into links:

A famous American scientist, Linus Pauling, started the modern craze for vitamin C as a cure-all.

If you do this, however, your readers may surf away to the Linus Pauling Wikipedia page (http://en.wikipedia.org/wiki/Linus_ Pauling) and may not return to your site. A more useful approach for citing sources is to put your links to sources at the end of your argument, the way scientific journals do. That way, readers will finish reading your argument and then visit your sources if they are interested.

Alternatively, you can design your links so that they appear in a new window. Your readers never really leave, so when they finish with the link and close the window, they're back on your site.

3.3c Categorical order: Any way you want it

Hypertext comes into its own when text is organized in categorical order. You have a subject that breaks more or less obviously into chunks, with no particular reason to list chunks in a specific order.

To spare your readers from navigation problems and information overload, you have to impose some kind of order on your categorical material. Maybe your site has a page with links to five other pages describing the five most popular trails in your regional park. You could list them from shortest to longest (or vice versa), from north to south, from easiest to hardest, even in alphabetical order. The blurb on the front page could indicate how you've organized them, from shortest to longest, for example:

Alpine Meadows Trail. 6 km. Really steep, but what views!

High Corniche Trail. 18 km. For experienced hikers only.

Readers will then use your blurb as a guide to the trails that most interest them.

3.4 Writing webtext from scratch

If you're simply transferring a print document (like a company report or a park brochure) to a website, imposing categorical order on your material will not be an issue.

But if you're generating your own text, you may feel baffled trying to sort it all out. You want to present coherent, easy-to-follow text, but your mind operates like simmering minestrone soup: ideas float to the surface, then sink again. Try to force organization on your own thoughts, and you get the cerebral equivalent of a system crash.

Clustering is one effective way to begin ordering your material. It's a simple process for outwitting yourself. Let the ideas of possible topics to include on your website come into your head in whatever order they like, and jot them down as they occur to you.

One idea inspires another; write that down too. Eventually you have several sheets of paper (or a computer screen) covered with ideas in no particular sequence.

Now that those ideas are out of your head, you can look at them and see which belong with which. Some are clearly introductory; others deal with the main subject; still others are part of the conclusion.

Cluster these ideas by tagging all the introductory items with a #1 or an A. The central ideas could be tagged #2, #3, #4, or B, C, D; the concluding ideas, #5 or E. If you're doing this exercise on a word processor, you can drag the ideas into the appropriate clusters, and before you know it you're organized.

Suppose you're putting together the website for Chesterton, a year-round sports and sightseeing destination. You might start jotting down ideas something like this:

history, skiing, snowboarding, zinc mine, logging, motels, hotels, youth hostels, regional parks, shopping, wildlife, environmental problems, swimming, water skiing, hiking trails, entertainment, restaurants

Obviously, some ideas inspired related ones, but most topics just occurred to you more or less at random. You see some obvious categories: Winter Sports, Summer Sports, Lodging. In the Winter Sports category, you could put skiing and snowboarding — and, come to think of it, you can also put in something about snowshoeing and ice skating.

Later on, you may want a separate page for Winter Sports, or you may decide to lump them in with other activities in a Year-Round Sports section.

Clustering works for almost any kind of writing task, and in webwriting it also suggests how you might design your navigation system. Maybe each section of your text will have its own navigation button on your front page. Or, if you're creating a long, scrolling page, a contents list at the top of the page could provide links to each section.

3.5 Style and display

You should be generating your webtext in whatever font and size are comfortable for you. Your readers may have set their machines to display some other default font, in some other size, and you can't control that. You also know that PCs and Macs may display your site somewhat differently. But you can ensure that your readers at least come close to seeing your text as you wish them to.

First, bear in mind that a serif font, like the one used in the main text of this book, is usually easier to read in extended text than a sans serif font, like the one used for headings throughout this book. However, some sans serif fonts like Verdana and Trebuchet were designed for the computer screen, and they work well also. So if you have long passages of text, a serif font (or a screen-designed font) is your best bet.

Point size makes a difference too. Usually, type should appear at no smaller than 10 points and no larger than 16 points. Readers with poor eyesight will especially prefer larger point sizes.

Stick with plain text. Use capital letters, small caps, italics, and boldface sparingly. The purpose of these special displays is to emphasize something; the more displays you use, the less emphasis anything will get. A whole paragraph in *italics* or SMALL CAPS or REGULAR CAPS will be hard to read.

Combining special displays only makes matters worse. A headline in ***BOLD ITALIC CAPS*** is overkill. If you must use all-uppercase letters, scale down the point size a little. Avoid underlining for emphasis; on the Web, an underline means a link.

Remember that a font like 12-point Georgia is great for reading on a monitor, but may be awkward as a printer font. For example, a table may not print completely because 12-point Georgia makes the table too big to fit on a letter-sized page.

A web author can specify a particular font and size right in the HTML code of the site. As long as the font is one that readers have on their computers, the site will appear more or less as the author wants it to. But if the font isn't there, the reader's default font will take over anyway — perhaps with disastrous results for display and readability. You should probably leave decisions about display up to your readers.

Be very careful about mixing colors. If you choose a black background and then display text in dark blue, you are going to make your site unreadable. The same is true of light colors, such as yellow text on a pale-green background. Good old black text on a white page should serve you well for most purposes. Your web-authoring program will usually let you specify the colors you want for your text and background. In general, your text should be as dark as possible and the background color (if any) should be pale.

Don't run text the full width of the monitor. A column about one-third to one-half the width of the screen is much easier to read because no line will be much more than ten words long. Any longer, and readers will have trouble finding the beginning of the next line.

3.6 Format for printing

Your readers may want to use your text both onscreen and on paper. Anyone who has tried printing from the screen, however, finds that not all documents look the same on paper. If you intend or expect your text to be used in both media, you can make readers' lives easier by avoiding certain practices:

- A wide multi-columned table can pack a lot of information into a single screen, but the reader's printer may not pick up the whole table (especially if the browser is set to display a big screen font and the reader hasn't remembered to switch to a printer font).

- Hyphenated words can make your screen text look tidy, but the hyphens may carry over into reformatted print text, where they become needless errors. Better to use a ragged-right margin with no hyphenations at all.

- Page number references usually become meaningless once a web page is printed out, as do navigation cues such as <u>Next</u> and <u>Back</u>.

When you are organizing your information and text, keep your readers in mind. If you know your site will get mostly hit-and-run readers, your pages will have to display concise chunks of text. If you're planning a library of long documents for readers looking for detailed information, then you won't have to edit yourself quite as harshly.

You will also have to consider how you want readers to respond to a particular item: with a click to some other chunk, or with an email answer? And will they get a suitable reward for their trouble? Webwriting, like chess, means you have to think several moves ahead — and put yourself in your readers' shoes.

3.7 Use bulleted lists

As readers, we're used to sentences on paper with long lists of nouns, verbs, and phrases. On the monitor such sentences become harder to read — and harder to respond to. This can be a problem in an interactive medium such as the Web.

Bulleted lists, used properly, can help convey information quickly and keep your readers on the page. Instead of plodding through long paragraphs, they can grasp the key points at once.

Bullets, then, have several functions for web writers:

- They focus attention on important points.
- They organize the content, often serving as a preview or summary of material.
- They improve the design of your page.

Compare the following almost unreadable paragraph with its bulleted form:

The media have given us some of their own occupational slang, like "sound bite," but trendy clichés usually come from the occupations and professions most interesting to the chattering classes. So business has given us bottom lines, deep pockets, and downsizing. The military has given us bite the bullet, in the trenches, breakthrough, and flak. Engineering gave us parameters, state of the art, leading edge, and reinventing the wheel. Athletics gave us team players, ballpark figures, level playing fields, and track records. Politics is the home of charisma, spin doctors, bandwagons, and momentum. The self-help movement gave us trendy clichés like self-actualizing, holistic, meaningful, one day at a time, and wellness.

The bulleted form:

The media have given us some of their own occupational slang, like "sound bite," but trendy clichés usually come from the occupations and professions most studied by the chattering classes:

- *Business:* bottom lines, deep pockets, downsizing

- *Military:* bite the bullet, in the trenches, breakthrough, flak

- *Engineering:* parameters, state of the art, leading edge, reinventing the wheel

- *Athletics:* team players, ballpark figures, level playing fields, track records

- *Politics:* charisma, spin doctors, bandwagons, momentum

- *Self-help movement:* self-actualizing, holistic, meaningful, one day at a time, wellness

Bulleted lists offer a couple of other advantages: You don't have to keep finding different ways to say the same thing (business has given us, the military has given us, athletics has given us), and it's easier to sound objective.

Keep bulleted lists parallel in form. That is, make every item a sentence ending in a period, or make every item a similar kind of phrase, without end punctuation.

Bulleted lists should be short. Six or seven bullets (as in the example above) are probably the maximum. One bulleted list per chunk or screen is enough.

Bulleted lists might introduce a longer discussion of the topics mentioned, or might provide links to other sites dealing with the topics.

Think about the length of the items in a bulleted list. If each item is actually a full paragraph, you're losing the impact of bulleting. Go to subheads instead. And if each item is just a single word, or a short phrase, the list should also have just three or four items.

And a small point: You have a huge number of bullet types to choose from: black circles, boxes, check marks, and so on. Keep your bullets simple and discreet.

 For an excellent guide to using bulleted lists, see Kim Long's *Writing in Bullets: The New Rules for Maximum Business Communication* published by Perseus Publishing.

---

4. Action: Communication Runs Both Ways

In Chapter 1, I talked about standard and interactive communication models. Many people still think the one-way standard model is the only one, and they use the standard metaphors (postal and ballistic) to describe what they do as communicators.

These metaphors are unfortunately still common in business and education. Teachers still "deliver" courses like so much junk mail, while politicians and businesses "target" voters and consumers with messages that "get through" like armor-piercing bullets. Governments launch cruise missiles at other governments to "send a message." The basic premise is that communication is a monologue, valuable only to the extent that it creates the desired effect.

If you design your website as a missile-launching platform aimed at passive readers, you're missing the whole point of the Web. No matter what you put on your site, it's worthless until readers arrive, construe your meaning, and act on your information (assuming you've made it possible for them to act).

Your readers, not you, will decide what your site really means and what value it has. You in turn have to respond to what your readers tell you, and before you know it, you're engaged in a conversation. If you listen to them and respond by adapting your content, you too are being interactive.

If you don't listen and don't adapt, your site is just a waste of time and bandwidth.

4.1 Response cues

Since the Web is supposed to be an interactive medium, your readers should respond to the information you provide with more than "So what?" You want them to take action.

Often, the only action needed for readers is to follow a link to another page, so the only response cue you need to provide is a clear link title and perhaps a blurb. But you may also want a more specific response: an email message, the submission of a form, a purchase order.

As marketers in the print media know, many people are slow and reluctant to respond on paper: They have to find a pen, and then an envelope, and then a stamp, and then they have to go out in the rain and mail their response. This is why so many companies provide stamped envelopes and some kind of bribe or threat — all simply to prod customers to respond.

Response is far easier on a website. Click on an email address and an email form pops up; just type in a few words, click on the Send button, and you're done. If typing is too much trouble, just reply to questions by clicking on the buttons of a form. Worried about transmitting your credit card number over the Web? Just provide your telephone number, and the organization you want to order from will call you.

Easy as response may be, most users still don't respond — especially if it means spending money. We'll look at marketing in more detail in Chapter 8, but for now, let's just put ourselves in the readers' shoes. What's in it for them if they email you, fill out your form, join your listserv, or answer your questionnaire? Presumably they get some sort of reward, a benefit or pleasure they would otherwise miss out on. And they have to know they'll miss it!

So invite your readers to act in their own interest:

Just fill out this form to make sure you get regular updates on Holly Cole's concert tour — plus a chance to win a copy of her latest CD!

To reserve your beautiful room at Chesterton Lodge — at 10 percent off this season's rates — just send us your telephone number and we'll call right back to get your credit card number and confirm your reservation.

If you want current news about the market for romances, you'll be glad you joined HEARTMART, the forum for professional and aspiring romance novelists. All you need to do is register (it's free!). At once you'll have access to market news and tips you can't find anywhere else!

This survey has 40 questions and takes only 10 to 12 minutes to complete. You'll be automatically entered into our contest for a free weekend at Chesterton Lodge.

You can make a difference! Let your government representatives know what you think by adding your name to our email protest. They'll know in minutes that you're angry and you want results!

Notice that each invitation tries to make action sound effortless: "Just fill out this form," "All you need to do," "They'll know in minutes." The action needed is built right into the appeal through a link to the suitable form. The Web is a culture of impatience, so effective appeals offer quick and painless ways to respond.

Exercise 3: Reviewing a Website

We usually understand a problem better (and find solutions faster) when we can discuss it in detail. If you look at your webtext in progress and all you can say is "This sucks!" you're not likely to improve it until you can identify the problem.

Reviewing someone else's site can help. The purpose of a website review is to enable you to identify the key elements of a site (both concept and execution) and, thereby, to identify what may help or hurt your own site.

You may want to develop your own review criteria, which could include some or all of the following:

- **Purpose.** Entertainment, marketing, information, or education? Is the purpose achieved? How? If not, why not — has the author misjudged the audience or misunderstood the nature and conventions of the Web?

- **Audience.** Novice or experienced? Young or old? Male or female?

- **Content.** Information-rich or just a jump page? Hit and run or archival? Does the content live up to the site title or blurbs? Is the text clear, well written, and well organized?

- **Appearance.** Good graphic sense? Do graphics enhance content or just decorate?

- **Accessibility.** Does the page load quickly?

- **Organization.** Is the site easily navigable? Does it require lots of scrolling? Lots of page jumps? Do you find "link rot" (links that go nowhere)? Is there any confusion about where <u>Back</u> or <u>Next</u> might lead?

If you can articulate your responses to good and bad websites, you'll be able to do the same for your own — and others who review your site will have more kind things to say about it.

Exercise 4: Converting Prose to Bullets

Convert the following paragraph to a bulleted list. Compare your version with the one in the appendix.

> Science fiction evolved from earlier genres and has kept some of their conventions. These include an isolated society, whether an island, a lost valley, or a distant planet; a morally significant language, such as Orwell's Newspeak; documents that play an important role in the story, like the Book of Bokonon in Vonnegut's Cat's Cradle; an ideological attitude toward sex, as in Huxley's Brave New World; and an inquisitive outsider, like Genly Ai in Le Guin's The Left Hand of Darkness.

[80 words]

4

WRITING GOOD
WEBTEXT

You have two main sources of material for your site: brand-new, self-created text, or text from other sources (e.g., annual reports, résumés, and technical memorandums). When you're importing text from print sources, you may have little choice: The site may simply be the archive of items that have to remain exactly as written. But in some cases, you may indeed have to adapt text from other sources to make it easily usable on your site.

Unless you've done very little writing for print, you're going to bring all kinds of habits from the print medium. That's fine; much of what goes on your site will end up on paper anyway, and the basics of good writing are the same in any medium.

Let's consider those basics in the light of the two information principles mentioned in Chapter 2:

- Clarity: Webwriting should be understandable at first glance.

- Correctness: Webwriting should reflect proper English usage and appropriate nonverbal messages.

To make sure that your writing is understandable at first glance, and that your writing is correct, consider the following suggestions.

1. Activate the Passive

The passive voice is an occupational hazard in many fields: science, technical specialties, academic writing, and bureaucracy are all rich sources of the passive voice. It's so common that most writers in such fields don't even know when they're using it — and if they do know, they're actually proud of themselves for doing so. They think they sound professional.

In the active voice, you always know who's doing what:

I studied the novels of Ursula K. Le Guin.

Pol Pot massacred hundreds of thousands of Cambodians.

Tim Berners-Lee invented the World Wide Web in 1989.

Most readers are very comfortable with the active voice, but in technical and bureaucratic writing, the active voice can draw attention to the writer or actor:

I tested 33 subjects for Ebola fever.

The inspectors found several minor infractions.

You made a serious mistake.

Technical and bureaucratic writers tend to avoid this kind of attention. They prefer to write:

Thirty-three subjects were tested for Ebola fever.

Several minor infractions were found.

A serious mistake was made.

This puts attention on the action, not the actors, and sometimes that's exactly what you want. It also appears more objective, because the actors disappear. At most, the actor turns up at the end of the sentence in a prepositional phrase:

Several minor infractions were found by the inspectors.

A serious mistake was made by you.

For writers who want to seem objective, and therefore more credible, the passive voice is dangerously attractive. That's because people who use passive voice a lot are likely to use it where it doesn't belong. Imagine your partner saying about your cooking: "Dinner was greatly enjoyed by me." Imagine yourself replying: "Your comments are very much appreciated." You'd both sound like stuffed shirts, and if you write your webtext the same way, your readers will think you really are a stuffed shirt — or at best a dull and wordy writer.

1.1 Don't confuse passive voice with past tense

If you write "I enjoyed dinner," you're using active voice and past tense. If you write "Dinner was enjoyed by me," you're still in past tense (dinner happened in the past), but you're in passive voice: The person who did the enjoying is lost in a prepositional phrase ("by me") at the end of the sentence, instead of being the subject at the beginning of the sentence.

Passive voice raises another problem for webwriters: it means more words. "I enjoyed dinner" is three words; "Dinner was enjoyed by me" is five. You are asking your poor reader to plow through two extra words for no good reason.

Sometimes, of course, you really do want to keep attention on the act, and not the actor. Maybe it's more important to mention that a mistake was made, without blaming anyone in particular. In those cases you should use passive voice — but use it consciously, when it serves your purpose, not just because you think it sounds professional.

2. Choose Concrete Anglo-Saxon Words

If you are conversant in English, you have the incredible luck to speak and write a language that falls in love with every other language it meets. English will borrow words from other languages all over the world, and then forget to return them.

English speakers weren't always so promiscuous (to use a Latin word). When Christianity first converted Britain, the Roman missionaries had to translate *crux* (cross) as *rood* because their converts preferred their own Germanic language. But when the French-speaking Normans conquered Britain, they imposed their Latin-based language on the country. So the French *croix*, from Latin *crux*, became the Modern English "cross." French and Latin were the languages of culture and law. Words from Anglo-Saxon Old English tended to stay in the mud of the barnyard.

We now have two main streams in English: words from the Latin (and Greek), which we use for technical, scientific, bureaucratic, and scholarly writing, and Anglo-Saxon words, which we use in everyday conversation.

Greco-Latin words tend to be abstract and hard to visualize. Anglo-Saxon words are concrete and easy to visualize. When we "cause collateral damage," it's hard to understand that we are "killing unlucky bystanders." In some cases, the Latin word has largely replaced the Anglo-Saxon one and we're stuck with the Latin. If we talk about "folks in North Carolina" instead of "people in North Carolina," we're going to sound a little too casual — even if "people" is Latin and "folks" is Anglo-Saxon.

On balance, though, Anglo-Saxon words are more immediate and understandable than Greco-Latin ones. Unless you're writing for highly specialized readers on a topic with a Greco-Latin technical vocabulary, choose the Anglo-Saxon word over the Greco-Latin one. (Most good dictionaries will list the origin of a word — OE means Old English, for example, and Gk means Greek. The definition may also give a more usable synonym for a rare word.)

3. Use Simple Sentences

Depending on their organization, sentences can be simple, compound, complex, or compound-complex. Here are examples of each:

- **Simple sentence**: This website celebrates the career of Holly Cole (subject: "site," verb: "celebrates").

- **Compound sentence:** This website celebrates the career of Holly Cole, and it also provides links to other Canadian singers' sites ("and" links to second subject, "it," and second verb, "provides").

- **Complex sentence:** This website celebrates the career of Holly Cole, who is a Canadian jazz singer (simple sentence with a subordinate clause attached — "who is a Canadian jazz singer"). A subordinate clause is one that can't stand on its own; it must be part of an independent clause, which is a complete sentence.

- **Compound-complex sentence:** This website celebrates the career of Holly Cole, who is a Canadian jazz singer, and it also provides links to other Canadian singers' sites (two independent clauses, linked by "and," with one independent clause modified by a subordinate clause).

You'll probably agree that the first sentence, the simple sentence, is the easiest to read. The longer a sentence becomes, the harder to read it becomes. Short, simple sentences will be much easier for everyone to understand quickly.

This is especially true of your home page, where many readers will first arrive. If that page is a solid mass of complex text, stretching clear across the screen, many readers will simply surf on to somewhere else. If your front page is just a brief introduction to the site's topics, plus a table of contents, simple sentences (and even phrases) are all you need.

Don't feel you have to write in a dumbed-down style, though. By all means vary your sentence patterns, if only to hold reader interest. But most sentences should be short and simple, with an average length of 20 words or so.

What if you're archiving long texts written in a complex style? Fine — your readers will probably want to download them to read later, either onscreen or as printouts.

4. Avoid Clichés

Avoid clichés like the plague. A cliché is a phrase or expression that was once so new and surprising that everyone repeated it. Like an unspoiled tourist destination ruined by too many tourists, the cliché loses its whole reason for existence when everyone uses it.

Clichés have several forms. Proverbial clichés include the stitch in time that saves nine, too many cooks spoiling the broth, and the ounce of prevention that saves a pound of cure. Sometimes you can get away with these by letting readers know that you know you're offering a stale but barely usable term: "Here's the proverbial ounce of prevention that will save you a pound of cure." This sentence may still be hard for people to understand if they've grown up with the metric system.

Slangy clichés have the embarrassing look of someone who thinks the 1970s are still happening. When you read terms like *uptight*, *outasight*, and *far out*, you're dealing with someone in a time warp (if that's not a cliché too).

If you're very careful you may be able to get away with dead slang if you use it ironically. "Kewl" for "cool" is an attempt to do so — though not a very successful attempt. (Scholars of slang may recall that before "cool" took over in the late 1950s, the "hepcats" described anything they really admired as "real George." That one, at least, died a merciful death.)

Trendy clichés are a little different. Slang tends to come from marginal groups like ethnic minorities; trendy clichés come from the mass media's journalists and commentators, the "chattering classes" (there's a trendy cliché in itself). People who write or speak for a living tend to use yet another cliché to drink each other's bathwater. One of them will come up with an unusual word or phrase, and everyone else seizes it. Before you know it, everyone on CNN or the editorial page of your local paper is talking about *interfaces*, *closure*, and *empowerment*.

When you look at a website, pay attention to the text. Does it resort to clichés or jargon? Of what kind? What is the effect created by the clichés or jargon? Can you imagine why the writer used them? And can you imagine how the text might read with the clichés removed?

You might try downloading text from a site and then revising it to remove all clichés. You're likely to find that your version is much stronger and more effective than the original.

Exercise 5: Identifying Clichés

In the following essay, circle all the words and phrases you've heard too often. Compare your choices (with those of your classmates if you're in school) and see where you agree or disagree.

At this point in time, comparing Canada's film industry with that of Hollywood is like comparing apples and oranges. Basically, if you're a Canadian filmmaker, you are caught between a rock and a hard place. To raise big bucks for a new project, you must go cap in hand with your dog-and-pony show to investors with deep pockets.

If you want these movers and shakers to see the big picture, you have to walk the walk and talk the talk. In estimating production costs, a ballpark figure isn't good enough for such hard-nosed, high-rolling wheelers and dealers. They're not impressed with smoke and mirrors. They've been around the block; they want to see the bottom line.

Getting a straight answer from these culturally deprived bean counters is like nailing Jell-O to the wall. They basically want a piece of the action that will let them milk a cash cow, but they refuse to throw money at the problem.

If you don't want to reinvent the wheel and go back to square one with some other potential backer, you had better have a good track record in your past history. Treat your backers with kid gloves, circle your wagons, and be ready to open the window of opportunity.

To make a major breakthrough, you need charisma, a holistic approach, a level playing field, and the ability to engage in meaningful dialogue. You must be incredibly credible. Cut to the chase: make your pitch like there's no tomorrow and you'll get two thumbs up going forward.

Basically, a simplistic Band-Aid approach won't work if you want the empowerment to finalize the deal and ink a contract. You need to stay on the leading edge and use state-of-the-art technology. Maybe the future looks like forty miles of bad road, but be prepared to tighten your belt and bite the bullet because that's the name of the game. You want to come up with a win-win situation, even if it means downsizing your original conceptualization. Otherwise, it's basically back to the drawing board.

When you've paid your dues in the film business, and you have a lot of irons in the fire, you can bring your pet project off the back burner. This could be your big self-actualizing experience, so give it your best shot. Otherwise you risk a loss of empowerment and a cash-flow problem.

Be sure your labor of love won't open a can of worms, or your game plan will go down the tubes. Take it one day at a time and go for the gusto. It's a no-brainer if you know where the bodies are buried, and you should be able to complete your project on time and under budget. Otherwise the in-vestors will look for a viable alternative while you experience déja vu all over again. And that's just the tip of the iceberg!

5. Choose Strong Verbs over Weak Ones

A hazard of business writing is the tendency to take a good, strong verb and turn it into a noun or phrase — and then to put a weak verb in its place. Consider the following:

Make a decision/Decide

Conduct a survey of/Survey

Make allowance for/Allow for

Make use of/Use

Do a review/Review

Perform a test/Test

The first phrases are longer, and may sound better to some people, but prefer the shorter ones unless you have some urgent reason to write longer. At least think about why the longer term would be better before you use it.

6. Be Aware of Dialect Variations

A dialect is a form of a language specific to a particular region that most local residents can generally understand, but which they may not use themselves. So a Scot from Edinburgh and an Australian from Melbourne will be able to converse in English, but they won't speak in the same accent or with quite the same vocabulary.

In different English dialects, the same word can mean different things. In American English, a *bluff* is a low cliff; in Canadian English as spoken in the prairie provinces, it means a grove of trees. And different words can mean the same thing. In Standard English, for example, *flaunt* means to show off, and *flout* means to break a rule in public.

Most North Americans, however, will talk about someone flaunting the law, but they don't mean waving the constitution around — they mean publicly breaking the law. In their dialects, that's what flaunt means. This may be incorrect Standard English, but it's perfectly understandable even to Standard English speakers.

The problem is that non-Standard usage may distract readers from the message. (In fairness, speakers and writers of Standard English may seem stuffy or pedantic to others. However, Standard remains the most widely understandable and accepted dialect.)

If you intend your website strictly for people who speak your own dialect, or you're trying for a strong local flavor, you can ignore Standard English. If you're trying to reach a broad audience, however, Standard English is your best choice. If you're unsure about what's considered Standard, countless manuals on English usage are available. Look in your library's reference section or a large local bookstore. Many dictionaries also include sections on grammar, spelling, and punctuation.

When in Doubt, Choose Plain Language

 For a quick and useful introduction to Plain Language, visit www.plainlanguage.gov — dedicated to making the US federal government understandable.

---

7. Be Precise

You may also mislead your readers by choosing a word that's not quite what you mean. Suppose you're writing text for the Chesterton website and you decide to put in a link to current weather reports and forecasts. Do you call it Chesterton Climate Report or Chesterton Weather Report?

Well, *climate* refers to weather conditions over a period of months or years; *weather* refers to what's going on at the moment. Chesterton may have a dry climate, but it may also be expecting a downpour tonight. Be sure to choose your words precisely.

At the same time, be aware that your readers may not be precise when they start searching for you. So while you should call it the Weather Report, you may also want to mention Chesterton's wonderful climate — because that's how some readers will search for your weather.

What if you find people often misspell a key search term? If that's a factor, put the misspelling in your invisible keywords (such as in your meta tags); the search engines will find it, but your visitors won't see it.

7.1 Diction: Choose your words carefully

Diction refers to the choice of words used to express an idea. Here are some words that may cause confusion if you choose them for the wrong purpose. Sometimes they sound like the term you want, or they've been misused so constantly that they sound right to you.

Adverse: harmful, negative. Some antibiotics cause adverse reactions in patients.

Averse: reluctant, opposed. She was averse to confronting her boss about the problem.

Affect (verb): to influence. This news will badly affect our share prices.

Effect (noun): result. This news had a bad effect on our share prices.

Aggravate: make worse. This news will only aggravate our image in the market.

Irritate: annoy. The board members were irritated by the bad news.

Alot: incorrect form of a lot. A lot of people make this mistake.

Allot: to divide or apportion. We can allot 50 seats on a first-come basis.

Allude to: suggest without naming. He alluded to his earlier successes.

Refer to: name directly. She referred to her best-selling Harry Potter books.

Alright: controversial form of All right. While it's widely used, purists resent it. No one will object to All right.

Ambiguous: having two or more meanings. Biweekly is ambiguous because it could mean twice a week or once every two weeks.

Ambivalent: having mixed or conflicting feelings. I feel ambivalent about challenging him on this issue.

Among: refers to three or more. The prize money was divided among the four winners.

Between: refers to two. The prize money was divided between the two winners.

Amount: refers to uncountable singular items. Feeding an army requires a large amount of flour.

Number: refers to plural items. Feeding an army requires a large number of trained cooks.

Apparently: presumably, by appearances. Since he didn't answer the door, he's apparently left the house.

Obviously: without doubt, plainly. Since we've searched the house, he's obviously left.

Assume: accept as a premise in an argument. Let's assume we bring in a flat tax.

Presume: take for granted. I presume his government will bring in a flat tax.

Assure: to promise. We can assure you of a great stay in our B&B.

Ensure: to make certain. You can ensure success by careful planning.

Insure: to guarantee against loss. Here's how to insure all your valuables with one policy.

Canvas: coarse cloth. The canvas sails were in shreds.

Canvass: to seek support. She will canvass the delegates on behalf of her candidate.

Cement: component of concrete; binding agent. Let's cement our agreement with a toast!

Concrete: hard material used for construction. The concrete overpass collapsed without warning.

Censor: to delete or suppress sensitive or dangerous information. The government censored reports from the battlefield.

Censure: to condemn or disapprove. The protestors censured the government's suppression of the news.

Cite: quote or summon. I can cite several authorities. They were cited for speeding.

Sight: to see or take aim. Dave Johnson sighted a UFO on April 2.

Site: location. This is a good site for links to Malaysian businesses.

Client: user of the services of a business or of a non-medical professional. As a client of Textor, you can expect the best in Web design.

Customer: person who buys from a store or business. As a customer of Self-Counsel Press, you're assured of prompt deliveries.

Climax: highest point, turning point in a story. The book's climax is deeply shocking.

Crescendo: growing in loudness or intensity. The crescendo of applause ended with a standing ovation.

Complement: to complete, or a total. This tie will complement your suit very well. The ship carries a complement of 32 crew members.

Compliment: to praise. I must compliment you on that elegant tie.

Compose: make or create. This committee is composed of six industry representatives.

Comprise: include or embrace. This committee comprises six industry representatives. (Note: Never say comprised of.)

Convince: to win an argument through appeals to logic and intellect. The experiment convinced even the skeptics.

Persuade: to win an argument through appeals to emotion. His tears and choked voice persuaded her of his sincerity.

Country: the territory of a nation. Canada is a very large country.

Nation: the people of a country. Canadians are a largely peaceable nation.

Dependant: a person who relies economically on another. My daughters are my dependants.

Dependent: variable, depending on. Our starting time will be dependent on the weather.

Desert: desolate, to abandon, or something deserved. The rocky desert stretched to the horizon. He deserted his companions. The king praised each knight according to his desert.

Dessert: a sweet. We had key lime pie for dessert.

Different from: used before a noun or pronoun. Taxco is different from Cuernavaca.

Different than: used before a clause. Taxco was different than I had expected.

Disc: correct spelling for all non-computer references: A compact disc, a herniated disc.

Disk: correct spelling for computer references: a ZIP disk, a floppy disk.

Disinterested: impartial, neutral. A disinterested arbitrator resolved the dispute.

Uninterested: not interested. The arbitrator was uninterested in minor issues.

Effective: having a desired result; coming into operation. The new policy, effective on Monday, should be an improvement.

Effectual: performing as desired. Her arguments were effectual in winning the debate.

Every day: each day. We record the air temperature four times every day.

Everyday: routine. Recording air temperature is an everyday activity for us.

Fewer: used with countable plural items. We've had fewer hits on our site this month than last month.

Less: used with uncountable singular items. We have less traffic on our site this month than last month.

Gibe: insult, mock. I'm tired of your asinine gibes.

Jibe: fit, agree. Your estimate jibes with ours.

Healthful: promoting good health. Vegetables form part of a healthful diet.

Healthy: in good health. She remained healthy and alert well into her 90s.

Hoard: a supply of something. We have a hoard of canned goods in the basement.

Horde: a large number of people. A horde of bargain-hunters swarmed into the shop.

Home in on: approach a desired goal. The pilot homed in on the radio beacon's signal.

Hone in on: incorrect but widespread usage; hone means sharpen, so the expression is meaningless.

Imply: suggest, hint. I don't mean to imply that the mistake was deliberate.

Infer: conclude, deduce. From the evidence, we can infer that the mistake was accidental.

Incidence: rate of occurrence. The incidence of drug-resistant tuberculosis is growing rapidly.

Incident: event. We've all learned from this unfortunate incident.

Irregardless: incorrect or humorous corruption of regardless.

Its: belonging to it. The committee has a lot on its agenda.

It's: contraction of it is or it has. It's going to be a long meeting. It's been raining all afternoon. (By the way, its' is not a word at all.)

Lead (verb) present tense. She can lead us to the crash site.

Led (verb) past tense. She led us to the crash site. (Don't confuse this with lead, the metal!)

Loath: reluctant, averse. He was loath to confront the problem.

Loathe: detest, hate. He loathes his adversaries.

Majority: More than 50 percent of a countable group. The majority of the delegates supported the motion.

Most: More than half of an uncountable item. We spent most of the afternoon snorkeling over the reef.

Moral: having to do with good and evil. We faced a painful moral decision.

Morale: group spirit. Morale in the office sank when we heard the news.

Perquisite: a special privilege (perk). A new car is one of the perquisites of the job.

Prerequisite: a condition or requirement. A BA is a prerequisite for admission to our program.

Principal: first or most important. My principal motive was to create a simple, elegant website.

Principle: rule or idea. We support the principle of free speech on the Web.

Proponent: advocate. She is a proponent of free speech on the Web.

Protagonist: central character in a story. Ged is the protagonist of Ursula K. Le Guin's Earthsea novels.

Reign: time of a monarch's rule. England prospered during the reign of Elizabeth I.

Rein: harness or control. Our teacher gave us free rein in the library.

Seasonable: appropriate to the season. Rainfall has been seasonable this summer.

Seasonal: pertaining to the season. We've broken the seasonal record for rain this summer.

Toe the line: conform. The soldiers formed even ranks by toeing the line.

Tow the line: incorrect usage, a misspelling of toe the line.

Waive: give up. You can waive your right to a jury trial.

Wave: move back and forth. Wave good-bye to your hard-won rights!

Weaved: past tense of weave meaning to avoid hitting something, or to contrive an involved story. The striker weaved through the defenders on his way to the goal. He weaved an incredible tale of adventure and derring-do.

Wove: past tense of weave meaning a fabric. Penelope wove endlessly at her loom.

In many of these cases, the difference between using the correct term and the incorrect one can be a spelling error that the spell checker on your computer will miss. That's also true of many other words: to, two, and too; there, their, and they're; coarse and course. Chances are you already know the words you have trouble with, so check them repeatedly against a dictionary until you're sure you're using them correctly.

8. Don't Use Extended Metaphors

In print text we may develop an argument through contrast and comparison — that is, by showing how two things are different or similar. Again we use transition words and phrases:

Unlike the dungeons, the castle's main floor is well furnished.

Just as in Cuernavaca, your hosts in Taxco will make you feel very welcome.

As Robert E. Horn advises in his book *Mapping Hypertext*, we can use such contrasts and comparisons only within a single section. The same is true of extended metaphors. In a print document, you might describe a government as a ship of state, with the executive as the bridge, the legislature as the engine room, and so on. This extended metaphor may work to help unify a passage of many paragraphs. But in hypertext, with readers skipping around in no predictable order, their first encounter with such a metaphor may be baffling.

9. Use Clear Antecedents

Hypertext must always include the antecedent for every pronoun in a given section. If I write, "She went on to earn a PhD in physics at MIT," I'd better mention her name earlier in the same section; otherwise readers won't know who "she" is.

10. Grammar and Usage: Common Errors

Whether you're in New Zealand or New York, chances are you make the same errors in Standard English. Here are some of the most common errors.

10.1 Sentence fragments

Your sentence will be a fragment if it lacks a subject or a verb. Here are some examples of fragments and their corrected versions:

Which surprised everyone.	This surprised everyone.
Really weird.	I think that's really weird.
A superb musician but a troubled human being.	She was a superb musician but a troubled human being.
Not bloody likely!	That's not bloody likely!

Sentence fragments are often fine in captions and blurbs, where the reader doesn't really need a full sentence. So a tag like "Joe Doakes in happier days" under a photo of Joe is all your readers require. A button linking to photos of your wedding can read

"The Big Day!" instead of "Come This Way to See Photos of Our Wedding Day."

However, in text where you're trying to explain or describe something in detail, avoid sentence fragments.

10.2 Subject-verb disagreements

Subject-verb disagreements are easy to make if you forget which word is your subject. For example:

The leader of the frightened soldiers were unable to make them cease firing.

Because "soldiers" is close to the verb, many people might make the verb plural ("were") to agree with it. But look again — it was the soldiers' leader, not the soldiers themselves, who couldn't make them stop firing. The correct verb should be singular ("was").

In other cases we have a compound subject but we mistakenly treat the two nouns like a single unit:

Snow and sleet makes hiking dangerous on these trails.

Spelling and grammar is my big problem in English.

In some cases, however, we really can treat a plural as a singular:

Six months is the standard probationary period.

A million dollars is still a lot of money.

Richards and Johnson is a distinguished legal firm.

And just to make things really confusing, sometimes we can describe a single thing or person with more than one noun and we still use a singular verb:

The lawyer and human-rights activist has enjoyed great success. (One person with two titles.)

The singer and songwriter has won a Grammy. (One person with two skills.)

If you're worried about subject-verb errors and you're not sure which noun is the subject, ask yourself: Who or what is performing the action of the verb in this sentence? Who's enjoyed success? Who's won two Grammys? The answer is your subject.

10.3 Incorrect pronouns

We use pronouns to stand in for nouns when repeating the nouns would sound awkward:

Dora released her latest video last month, and she says she's happy with it.

Imagine using Dora four times in that sentence:

Dora released Dora's latest video last month, and Dora says Dora's happy with it.

We sometimes run into trouble when we forget that some pronouns are subjective (that is, they perform the action of the verb in the sentence) and others are objective (they receive the action of the verb).

He emailed her. She emailed him.

We'd laugh if we read:

Her emailed he. Him likes she a lot.

But many people, in conversation and in writing, will say:

She emailed him and I.

Me and her went to the conference.

Her and her husband set up a home-based business.

Evidently they think that the rules don't apply if they're talking about more than one person! But the rules do apply:

She emailed him and me.

She and I went to the conference.

She and her husband set up a home-based business.

Another pronoun problem is *myself*, which some people use incorrectly. Pronouns with "self" are either reflexive or emphatic:

I asked myself a question (action of verb turns back on the asker).

I myself told you it wouldn't work (emphasizes who told you).

Don't use myself as a long-winded way to say I or me:

Joan and myself went to the conference.

My wife and myself set up a home-based business.

10.4 Misuse of adjective for adverb

Adjectives modify nouns: a *good* man, a *fast* computer. Adverbs modify verbs, adjectives, and other adverbs: a *truly* good man, a *really* fast computer. Sometimes you can change the meaning of a sentence by using (or misusing) some common adjectives: "You did good by winning the contest" is incorrect, but "You did good by raising flood-relief money" is correct. We do well when we perform with style and excellence. We do good when we make the world a better place.

These are just four common grammar and usage problem areas. For details on these and many other hazards of usage, spelling, and punctuation, consult almost any composition handbook or dictionary.

Exercise 6: Activating the Passive

Revise these sentences to activate the passive voice and then check your answers against those in the back of the book.

1. It is argued by some researchers that alien bodies were retrieved by the US Air Force from a crashed spacecraft near Roswell, New Mexico, in 1947.

Exercise 6: Continued

2. Miles Davis's Sketches of Spain was hailed by critics as one of his finest works.

3. The graphic user interface was originally developed by researchers at Xerox.

4. A cholera outbreak in 19th-century London was stopped when a neighborhood water pump's handle was removed by a local physician.

5. These graphics have been chosen carefully to illustrate each step of the process.

Exercise 7: Using Anglo-Saxon Vocabulary

Replace each of the following words with an Anglo-Saxon word or phrase (or a more common Greco-Latin word):

1. Altercation

2. Antagonist

3. Capitulate

4. Celestial

5. Demotic

6. Epitome

7. Fiduciary

8. Gravamen

9. Impediment

10. Litigious

If you can't find a shorter, clearer word without checking your dictionary, imagine how your readers would feel if they didn't have a dictionary at all. Now that you know these words, do your readers a favor: Don't use them in your webtext!

5

EDITING WEBTEXT

In ancient Rome, the title of the person who sponsored a gladiatorial fight to the death was Editor. Maybe because of that association with hacking and slashing, modern writers are often suspicious of editors. They shouldn't be. A good editor can save you from countless embarrassing mistakes while helping you make your points more coherently, more eloquently, and even more gracefully.

What's more, you can be your own editor. Here are some steps you can take to improve your own text once you've drafted it.

1. Don't Trust Your Spell Checker

Computer spell checkers are rubber crutches; they fail just when you need them most. All they do is compare what you've written with a list of words, and if they find the word in their list, they say it's okay. So you may have written their when you meant to write there, or your when you meant you're, and the spell checker will tell you it's correct.

The spell checker will of course catch outright typos, doubled words, and other errors, so it has some usefulness. But a quick skim of your document, flagging obvious goofs, is the best you can hope for from a spell checker.

If you have a grammar and style checker, you're a little better off, but not much. Style checkers can spot bad habits like overuse of the passive voice, or too many prepositional phrases. This at least forces you to think about whether you have to indulge in such habits.

2. Check Your Reading Level

Your style checker can also give you a sense of the reading level of your text. It does so by counting the number of syllables per word, the number of words per sentence, and the number of sentences per 100 words. The reading level, usually expressed as a grade level, goes up as words, sentences, and paragraphs get longer. (This book is readable at the Flesch-Kincaid grade 7 level, for example.)

If your site is aimed at a general audience, especially one including young children or persons who don't read English fluently, it's common sense to keep the reading level as low as the subject permits. You don't get extra points for making your text readable only to PhD candidates.

Clearly you don't want to dumb down your text needlessly, but a lower reading level makes your text understandable to more people. And the point of a website, after all, is to make information available to as many people as possible.

I got a powerful lesson about readability a few years ago when I typed a chapter from the book of Ecclesiastes into a Word file and then checked its readability. Even with its verses compounded into two- and three-sentence paragraphs, Ecclesiastes came out readable at the grade 3 level.

How readable are you?

For a really detailed analysis of your text, go to Readability.info www.readability.info). You can either upload a Word file, or enter the URL of your website. You'll get seven different readability scores, with an explanation of them.

Readability.info also gives you the number of sentences and their length, and the number of paragraphs plus number of sentences in the average paragraph. This can help you identify unconscious writing habits.

3. Cut Verbiage

Your hit and run text is all that most of your readers will bother with. Only the really dedicated people will actually look at your archived text and perhaps download it for careful reading. Therefore your hit and run text should be as brief as possible, so it delivers its message clearly and quickly.

If you set yourself an arbitrary word limit — for example, no chunk of text may run over 75 words — you will be amazed at how easy it is to cut the fat out of your text.

As a first step, deliberately write long chunks of text: maybe 150 or 200 words. Then start cutting words until you're down to 55 or 60 words. Now you have the luxury of actually adding some words. Every sentence, every phrase, every word has had to fight for its life. Nothing is there just because it sounds good — you're writing, remember, not making music! You've packed the maximum meaning into the minimum text, so your readers will get the message in the shortest possible time.

4. Critique Your Own Text

A writer lives inside your head, and so does an editor. They don't always get along. Your inner writer is having a great time being creative; your inner editor is watching over the writer's shoulder and groaning. While the writer is cranking out Great Prose, the editor is in despair about what drivel this all is.

The writer doesn't hear the details, but starts feeling nervous: Maybe this isn't all that good after all. Finally the writer decides something's gone horribly wrong (heaven knows what) and abandons the job.

Sound familiar?

It doesn't have to be that way. If you were a best-selling author, you could send your messed-up manuscript to your high-priced editor, who would tell you exactly what was going right and wrong with the manuscript and offer detailed advice on improvements. What if you don't have the services of a professional editor? Well, you have an editor living right inside your skull — all you have to do is give that editor a chance to put criticisms into words.

So as you're putting your webtext together, keep a diary or journal in which you can make notes to yourself about how your writing is going. If a problem does arise, your inner editor can sound off about it ("The introduction is way too long and too cute, and we don't need to use the word *fiduciary*").

Once you've put the problem into words, something startling happens: The solution follows almost instantly. When you start organizing your ideas into sentences and paragraphs, the process seems to free the creative part of your mind, and it comes up with answers that you'd never get if you just pounded your head against the edge of your desk. Sometimes the answer comes before you've finished writing the sentence describing the problem.

Self-critiques don't just help with problems of style. Your inner editor may also warn you about problems in the organization of your whole site. Maybe you want to list a bunch of excellent links to other sites on your front page; your editor, if given the chance, will tell you not to be an idiot: Put them down in the basement so readers don't find them until they've looked at all our own stuff.

5. Print Out to Proofread

You simply cannot trust your own proofreading abilities unless you proofread from paper. Not only is computer-screen text hard to read, it's hard to proofread as well. That means real trouble for you as a webwriter: Your text may look sub-literate even if only mistyped, but it will be very hard for you to catch your typos if you're proofreading only on the screen. The longer you try, the less accurate you'll be because monitor reading will tire you out. Your readers, however, will come to your site fresh and unfamiliar with your text. So they'll spot those typos every time.

Sections that you haven't changed much are especially dangerous. On my first website, I didn't look at my headline after I'd written it; when I installed the site, the headline featured an embarrassing typo — which I didn't catch until after I'd invited dozens of colleagues to take a look.

When you print out your site text to proofread it, don't print it out in 10-point single-spaced text. Make it 14-point and double-spaced, use an unfamiliar font, and let it sit overnight before you proofread. That way your text will look unfamiliar. You'll have to read what's actually on the paper, not what's on the inside of your forehead — and errors are more likely to leap out at you.

Here's another useful tip: Read your text out loud. That will also force you to read every word, instead of just skimming. You may find some awkward phrases that looked okay on the screen and on paper, but that sound clumsy or suggest an unintended meaning. Better to catch them now.

Does this sound like a lot of hassle for a humble little web page about your favorite singer or your dog-walking service? Maybe so, but typos, bad grammar, and other mechanical errors can really hurt the impact of your page. Maybe you can create amazing sounds and graphics, but if you can't spell, your readers will notice — and they won't like it.

This is especially true when you have a business site promoting either your own skills or the virtues of the company that's hired you to write content for its site. Simple proofreading mistakes instantly make you look bush-league and unprofessional.

6. Don't Respect the Text!

Maybe it's an ingrained respect for the written word going back to ancient Babylon when only the sacred priests were literate. Maybe it just goes back to the days of the manual typewriter, when a minor error or afterthought meant re-typing the whole page.

Whatever the reason, we revere text too much. It gives us a deadly dangerous readiness to dump print-for-paper onto a website and think we've done our job.

Respect for text is bad enough for print-media writers; on the Web, it's disastrous. In print, we expect readers to skip right along from point to point. If our text is wordy or complex, we rely on readers to get the point pretty quickly anyway. Maybe we even tell ourselves that our ideas are so subtle and nuanced that only an elaborate style will convey them adequately.

On the Web, readers need only hit the back button to dismiss our illusions. If we want to attract them, hold them, and inspire them to react to what we've said, we need to look at our text with a cold, dispassionate eye.

Jakob Nielsen tells us the computer monitor slows down reading speed by up to 25 percent, but we haven't yet accepted the implication: that everything we adapt from print to Web should be at least 25 percent shorter. Print-media text assumes readers will sit still for a long, interwoven argument; when Web surfers find such arguments, too often they just surf on to somewhere else. And when that happens we've squandered the great advantage the Web gives us as writers: the chance to engage our readers in dialogue.

Some print materials, of course, don't need adaptation because they're simply archived on the site. An annual report, a survey, an article once published in a newspaper — these can remain at full length. As PDF (portable document format) files, they can even retain their original formatting.

But for visitors who are simply scanning your site, you should try to provide a kind of smorgasbord, with everything available at a glance. To make scanning easier, you need to adapt most print texts by including:

- Self-explanatory titles on your contents pages, so scanners will know what they're heading for when they click through.

- Blurbs, in case the titles really aren't all that self-explanatory.

- Headings that either form titles for individual chunks of text, or divide even a single screenful of text into two or three segments.

- Condensed text that conveys the key elements as concisely as possible — perhaps with links to the original-length archived item for those who want every detail.

The condensation process demands the most disrespect for print-source text. A useful guideline is to cut such text by not just 25 percent, but 50 percent, just to see if it's possible. If the result can't stand on its own, then restore some of the original text (or a concise version of it) until a scanner, arriving directly on this chunk, will understand what it's about.

And not only understand it — respond to it! Maybe you want your readers to respond by jumping to the archived original, or emailing your organization, or buying the product. Whatever the response desired, the text should make it an easy, attractive choice. What's more, the choice itself should spark a positive response from the website:

Congratulations! Your first email newsletter is on its way! Let us know what you think of it.

Thank you for your purchase. It should reach you within 48 hours. Meanwhile, your user manual is already in your mailbox.

Maybe you feel awkward about disrespecting the text, but what's really important is that you give utmost respect to the visitors who have honored you with their presence on your site. Whatever you can do to make their visit interesting, surprising, and successful — including presenting text as clearly and concisely as possible — should make it clear that their needs come first.

7. Edit for International Readers

When you write for the Web, remember that it really is worldwide. Many readers may be native English speakers, but most Web users are not. Even native speakers may have trouble with particular dialects. For example, a car smash in Memphis is a fender bender in California. When an Australian man has a mate, it's his male friend and not his wife. If you have the exformation about such usages, they're not a problem. But international readers may not have that exformation at all.

If we're going to meet the needs of those readers, we have to make our language as simple and clear as possible. This isn't easy. Recently I asked a Chinese pen pal for her snail mail address. She sent me her Hotmail address instead ... because she thought *snail mail* must mean an email account that opens very slowly.

Does this mean that we have to set our grammar checkers to flag anything that might make a third-grader frown? Do we have to define every word?

No — at least, not usually. The other day I referred a foreign student to my college's website for advice about admissions and fees. The information for foreign students isn't written very simply. After all, if its readers can't understand routine college-level English, they're not yet ready for us.

Similarly, foreign professionals may be very much at ease with the technical English of their profession, even if their colloquial English is awkward. So a technical site need not oversimplify its content.

In some cases, you may even want to emphasize your dialect. A Canadian site can offer an exotic flavor to American visitors if its writers labor to spell British-style. It can also use distinctly regional Canadian terms, like saltchuck for salt water and bluff for grove of trees. If your site's dialect is likely to baffle too many visitors, a glossary may help.

Many readers will grasp unfamiliar terms just from context, but the context can be blunt or subtle:

> We went out on the saltchuck, which is what some British Columbians call salt water.

> We went out on the saltchuck, braving choppy waves in our sea kayaks.

So for technical sites, or "exotic sites," specialized dialects will be fine. A site designed for general readers, however, should probably stick to bare-bones Standard English — a vocabulary of widely understood words with very few regional, slangy, or idiomatic expressions.

Am I being a terrible spoilsport who disapproves of having fun with English? I should hope not! But it should be fun that your readers will understand and appreciate.

And don't forget one priceless advantage you have as a webwriter — you can encourage and provoke your readers to ask questions about the unusual words and phrases on your site. Your content isn't just a take-it-or-leave-it box lunch, but a constantly changing buffet of interesting and sometimes mysterious items. If customers find you eager to explain what's on offer, they'll be delighted to learn and experiment — and you'll learn how much you still have to learn about your own language.

8. A Webwriter's Style Guide

Several style guides already exist for the Web, though they're more honored in the breach than the observance. Sir Tim Berners-Lee, the father of the Web, created such a style guide. So did Gareth Rees, whose guide is available in the electronic appendix to this book (at www.crofsblogs.typepad.com).

In the print media, style guides don't interest rank amateurs or literary geniuses. Amateurs don't know the rules; geniuses break them. But for professional writers, style guides are as necessary as tape measures and plumb bobs are for carpenters. This is especially true if you're responsible for designing and maintaining a corporate or advocacy site where both appearance and language should be correct and consistent.

With millions of pages up on the Web now, it really helps when websites imitate one another. New visitors don't have to spend time learning the quirks of each particular site, including language quirks.

Your style guide can therefore be descriptive, telling your readers, "This is the way most people say it." That's especially true for sites catering to specialized audiences with their own dialect or technical shoptalk.

But other style guides should be prescriptive, laying down the law on everything from abbreviations to precise word usages. Newspapers and publishers use such guides for the sake of consistency, and to save their writers and editors from repeatedly researching every obscure question. I can recommend several for North American webwriters:

USA:

The Chicago Manual of Style (15th edition). University of Chicago Press, 2003. Website: http://www.press.uchicago.edu/Misc/Chicago/cmosfaq/cmosfaq.html

The Associated Press Stylebook and Libel Manual. Norm Goldstein, ed. Perseus Press, 1998.

The Microsoft Manual of Style for Technical Publications (2nd edition). Microsoft Press, 1998

Canada:

CP Stylebook: A Guide for Writers and Editors, 14th edition, ed. Peter Buckley. Canadian Press, 2006.

The Canadian Style: A Guide to Writing and Editing. Dundurn Press, 1997.

Editing Canadian English, 2nd edition. Macfarlane Walter & Ross, 2000.

Guide to style guides

 See Jeffrey Zeldman's style guide for A List Apart (www.alistapart.com/contribute/styleguide) for an example of how to specify everything from the use of metaphors to the use of commas.

For an example of a style guide for a newspaper's blog, see Telegraph blogging style guide at http://blogs.telegraph .co.uk/upload/may06/styleguide.htm. And the BBC News Styleguide (www.bbctraining.com/pdfs/newsstyleguide.pdf) should be helpful also. *The Economist* offers a style guide at www.economist.com/research/styleguide/.

Do guides simply impose print standards where they don't belong? Such guides set limits to expression in a medium that — in theory — requires no such limits at all. Some might even argue that style guides force newcomers to adopt the vocabulary and tone of the Web's privileged early adopters.

I doubt it. Mavericks are still free to ignore (or attack) "correct" style in their preferred Web genres. But for the vast majority of users, consistent style within Web genres is as critical as consistent navigation.

What follows is a brief guide mixing both descriptive and pre-scriptive. I've emphasized Web-related expressions and terms that may be useful for both native English speakers and those for whom English is a foreign language. Some usages are standard whether in print or in webtext, and ignoring such usage will only distract or confuse your readers.

Web jargon and slang can be especially baffling to newcomers, whether English is their native language or not. In other cases, an expression that seems vivid and fresh to you may be baffling or boring to others. In such cases, you should at least think carefully before using them.

8.1 Abbreviations

We use short forms of many words and phrases. Some are true abbreviations, while others are acronyms or initialisms. CA and Calif. are both abbreviations of California. UNESCO (United Nations Educational, Scientific, and Cultural Organization) is an acronym; we pronounce it as a word.

Sometimes acronyms become acceptable as words themselves, like scuba (self-contained underwater breathing apparatus) and radar (radio detection and ranging). FBI (Federal Bureau of Investigation) and RCMP (Royal Canadian Mounted Police) are initialisms; we sound out each letter.

Some abbreviations may be so common that they need no explanation: UN, NATO, TNT. Even then, if you expect numerous international readers unfamiliar with English abbreviations, an explanation somewhere in your text may be helpful. If you feel you must use an abbreviation that your readers may not recognize, write out the whole term first before beginning to use the abbreviation:

He joined the National Research Council (NRC) in 1986.

In some cases, the abbreviation may need more than just a spelling-out. TNT stands for trinitrotoluene; better to say TNT, a powerful explosive. This is especially true for abbreviations from other languages:

Pemex, Mexico's national oil corporation.

Acronyms formed only from the initial letters should be all capitals: North Atlantic Treaty Organization = NATO. (However, British usage allows Nato.) Acronyms formed from initials and other letters in a proper name take capitals and lower case letters:

National Biscuit Company = Nabisco. Acronyms formed from phrases don't take capitals: microwave amplification by stimulated emission of radiation = maser, radio detection and ranging = radar.

Unless a Greek or Latin abbreviation is universally used, prefer the English equivalent. Your reader will understand "that is" and "for example" much faster than "i.e." and "e.g."

Here are some common abbreviations, together with their complete forms and their meanings. In many cases, when such abbreviations appear in text intended for a website, your readers will thank you if you translate them into plain English.

8.2 Business abbreviations

acct or a/c	account
AG	Allgemeine Gesellschaft, general company Aktiengesellschaft, joint stock company (German)
ARM	adjustable rate mortgage
ASAP	as soon as possible
assn./assoc.	association
ATM	automated teller machine
atty.	attorney
bal.	balance
Bcc.	blind carbon copy
b.l., b/l, B/L	bill of lading
CEO	chief executive officer
CFO	chief financial officer
CIO	chief information officer
c/o	care of

CPS	certified professional secretary
ctn.	carton
CY	calendar year
cc, Cc	carbon copy
Cia.	compañía, company (Spanish)
Cie.	compagnie, company (French)
co., Co.	company
c.o.d.	cash (paid) on delivery
CPA	certified public accountant
dba	doing business as
dis.	discount
dtd.	dated
ea.	each
EEO	equal employment opportunity
EOM	end of month
Ext., ext.	telephone extension (for example, Ext. 337)
FAX, fax	facsimile copy
FOB, f.o.b.	free on board (delivered without charge to buyer)
frt.	freight
fwd.	forward
FY	fiscal year
FYI	for your information
GATS	General Agreement on Trade in Services
GATT	General Agreement on Tariffs and Trade

GDP	gross domestic product
G.M.	general manager
GmbH	Gesellschaft mit beschrankte Haftung (German for limited liability company)
GNP	gross national product
hdlg.	handling
HR	human resources
HRD	human resources department
ID	identification
inc., Inc.	incorporated
inst.	instant (the present month)
IOU	I owe you
LCL	less than a carload lot
LLC	limited liability company
Ltd.	Limited (stockholders' liability limited to size of their investment)
Ltée	Limitée (French for limited liability)
max.	maximum
mdse.	merchandise
mfr.	manufacturer
min.	minimum
MIS	management information systems
misc.	miscellaneous
mo.	month
NAFTA	North American Free Trade Agreement

pd.	paid
PLC, plc	public limited company (British equivalent of US corporation)
Pty	proprietary
qty.	quantity
R&D	research and development
RE, Re, re	regarding, concerning
recd., rec'd	received
rept.	report or receipt
RSVP	please reply
S.A.	sociedad anónima/société anonyme (Spanish & French for anonymous society, like limited liability)
SOP	standard operating procedure
Spa, SpA	Societá per Azione (Italian for corporation)
Srl	Societá a responsabilitá limitata (Italian for limited responsibility, like limited liability)
treas.	treasurer
VP	vice-president
whsle.	wholesale

8.3 Business symbols

%	percent (out of 100)
$	dollar(s)
¢	cent(s)
£	British pound
¥	Japanese yen

°	degree(s) (temperature or angle)
=	is equal to
≠	is not equal to
#	number (before a numeral — #10)
#	weight in pounds (after a numeral — 10#)
'	feet (6' tall)
"	inches (6'2" tall)
"	ditto (exactly equal; the same)
"	minutes (subdivision of degrees of latitude and longitude)
¶	paragraph
§	section
x	by (11"x14"); multiplied by (3x5)
™	Trademark
®	Registered
©	Copyright

8.4 Email abbreviations

By definition these are more likely to turn up in email than on websites, but you should be familiar with some of these abbreviations if only because they may turn up in the email that your site inspires.

AFAIK	as far as I know
BBIAB	be back in a bit
BFD	big XXX deal
BRB	be right back
BTW	by the way

FAQ	frequently asked questions
FWIW	for what it's worth
FYI	for your information
G, <G>	grin (placed after a joke or a remark intended as such)
GD&R	grinning, ducking, and running (after a humorously intended insult)
GD&R,VVF	grinning, ducking, and running, very, very fast
IANAL	I am not a lawyer (but...)
IIRC	if I recall correctly
IMNSHO	in my not so humble opinion
IMO	in my opinion
IMHO	in my humble opinion
IOW	in other words
LMAO	laughing my ass off
LOL	laughing out loud
OIC	oh, I see
OTOH	on the other hand
PITA	pain in the ass
ROTFL	rolling on the floor laughing
RTFM	read the XXX manual
SYSOP	system operator (manager of a bulletin board or online forum)
TIA	thanks in advance
TIC	tongue in cheek

TTFN	ta-ta for now	
TTYL	talk to you later	
VBG, <VBG>	very big grin	
WRT	with regard to	
WYSIWYG	what you see is what you get	
YMMV	your mileage may vary	

8.5 Greek and Latin

A.D.	Anno Domini	Year of our Lord
a.m., A.M.	ante meridiem	before noon
anon.	anonymous	nameless
c. or ca.	circa	about (a date)
cf.	confer	compare
e.g.	exempli gratia	for example
et al.	et alii	and other persons
etc.	et cetera	and others, and so on
et seq.	et sequens	and the following
fl.	floruit	flourished
ib., ibid.	ibidem	in the same place
i.e.	id est	that is
lb.	libra	pound
loc. cit.	loco citato	in the place cited
n.b.	nota bene	note well
ob.	obiit	died
op.	opus	work

op. cit.	opere citato	in the work cited
PhD	Philosophiae Doctor	Doctor of Philosophy
p.m., P.M.	post meridiem	afternoon
pro tem	pro tempore	temporarily
P.S.	post scriptum	written afterward
pseud.	pseudonym	false name
Q.E.D.	quod erat demonstrandum	which was to be demonstrated
q.v.	quod vide	which see
R.I.P.	requiescat in pace	rest in peace
v.	vide	see
viz.	videlicet	namely
v., vs.	versus	against

8.6 Scholarly/general abbreviations

Note that most lowercase and mixed abbreviations take periods. Mixed abbreviations that begin and end with a capital letter don't take periods.

AA	associate in arts (two-year degree)
AS	associate in science (two-year degree)
BA, AB	bachelor of arts
BBA	bachelor of business administration
B.Comm.	bachelor of commerce
BS, B.Sc.	bachelor of sciences
bbl.	barrel(s)

BTU	British Thermal Unit (heat required to raise temperature of 1 pound of water by 1 degree Fahrenheit)
C.	Celsius, Centigrade
DA	doctor of arts
DBA	doctor of business administration
DD	doctor of divinity
DDS	doctor of dental surgery/dental science
cwt.	hundredweight (100 pounds)
deg.	degree, degrees
doz.	dozen
ed.	editor, edited
EdD	doctor of education
est.	estimated
f., ff.	and the following (pages)
hp	horsepower
JD	doctor of jurisprudence
JM	master of jurisprudence
Jr.	junior (the son of someone with the same name)
JSD	doctor of the science of laws
ll.	lines
LLB	bachelor of laws
MA	master of arts
MBA	master of business administration

MD	doctor of medicine
MS, M.Sc.	master of science
MS, ms., mss.	manuscript(s)
n.d.	no date given
NGO	non-governmental organization
No., no.	numero (number)
n.p.	no numbered pages
obs.	obsolete
p., pp.	page(s)
P.Eng.	professional engineer
PhD	doctor of philosophy
quango	quasi-autonomous non-governmental organization
SJ	Society of Jesus
ThD	doctor of theology
vol.	volume

8.7 Web abbreviations

For detailed definitions, consult the following websites:

- Webopedia: www.webopedia.com

- Netlingo: www.netlingo.com

- Jargon File Resources:
  www.tuxedo.org/~esr/jargon/jargon.html

CGI	Common Gateway Interface; allows interaction between users and websites through forms, orders, and other responses

FAQ	Frequently Asked Questions; usually covers points raised by newcomers; pronounced fack
HDML	handheld device markup language; formats content for Web-enabled mobile phones
HTML	hypertext markup language; code that tells a browser how to display text, graphics and other elements of a Web page
HTTP	hypertext transfer protocol
IP	Internet Protocol; a server address, often four numbers separated by dots: 123.45.678.910
MP3	MPEG audio layer 3; coding scheme for compressing audio files. MPEG stands for Motion Picture Experts Group.
PDF, pdf	portable document format (readable with Adobe Acrobat on any computer)
S-HTTP	Secure HTTP; sends an individual message in a secure, encrypted form
SSL	Secure Sockets Layer; encrypts data in multiple messages
TCP/IP	Transmission Control Protocol/Internet Protocol; basic software needed to connect to the Internet
URL	uniform resource locator; the address of a particular website
WAP	Wireless Application Protocol; allows access to Web information over mobile phones, pagers, other devices
WML	Wireless Markup Language; an XML language used with WAP devices
XML	extensible markup language; an advanced Web language that allows designers to create their own tags to define, validate and interpret data

8.8 Punctuating abbreviations

Frequently used abbreviations tend to lose their periods — B.A. becomes BA, and U.S.A. becomes USA — but it's still correct to include them. As noted earlier, abbreviations with mixed capital and lower-case letters usually keep their periods. Mixed abbreviations that begin and end with capitals lose their periods. (Geographical abbreviations used in postal addresses should not include periods, however, because postal scanners have trouble with them. So postal mail addressed to British Columbia or California should display BC or CA with no punctuation.)

An honorific or title before a name is usually abbreviated (in North America, with a period; in Britain, without) when the person's whole name is included:

Prof. Zhu Minhua, Maj. Gen. Robert Smith, Mr. David Porter, Ms. Joan Acosta. (But Ms. often appears as Ms even in North America.)

A title does not appear before a name if a title follows the name:

Louise Fairfax, MD; John Hutchinson, PhD.

When a sentence ends with an abbreviation including periods, only one period is needed:

Welcome to B.C.

When a sentence ends with a question mark or exclamation mark, it follows the last period of the abbreviation:

Welcome to B.C.!

8.9 Pluralizing abbreviations

Simply add s to most abbreviations: MVPs (most valuable players), MIAs (soldiers missing in action), NGOs (nongovernmental organizations).

8.10 Abbreviating dates

International and governmental organizations tend to display dates as year/month/day: 2006/03/21 is March 21, 2006. Most people, however, prefer day/month/year (21 March 2006) or month/day/year (March 21, 2006). From 2001 to 2031, abbreviated dates may be ambiguous: does 03/04/05 mean April 5, 2003, March 4, 2005, or April 3, 2005?

To ensure understanding, write out dates in full or use abbreviations for the names of months: Apr 3 2005, 5 Apr 2003.

Abbreviations of calendar eras usually appear as:

AD: Anno Domini

BC: Before Christ

BP: Before the present (generally taken to be AD 2000 — so 6400 BP = 4400 BC)

BCE: before the common era

CE: common era

These last two terms recognize that not everyone using the Christian calendar is necessarily a Christian.

8.11 Biased terms

As a webwriter you may want to challenge your readers, but challenges shouldn't include gratuitous pokes in the eye. Terms that seem perfectly natural to you may be deeply offensive to others. Is that because you're OK and your readers are thin-skinned idiots? Or because you don't have enough respect for your readers to address them in a civil manner?

Concern with political correctness can lead to euphemism and denial of reality. But I suggest that when you can use a term that doesn't bother your readers, you should choose it — especially if they themselves prefer the term. One happy result of this choice is likely to be better writing.

For example, the stereotyping that drives people crazy is sloppy writing that reflects (and promotes) sloppy thinking. Generalizations about any group — dumb college athletes, bad women drivers, violent teenagers, noisy American tourists — will invariably collapse under any serious examination.

So your webtext should avoid such generalizations, whether you're tempted to make them about nationalities, ethnic groups, demographic groups, or any other class of people. Remember the "you" attitude: It's your website, but it's really about your visitors, not you.

More specifically, consider the following guidelines for avoiding biased terms.

8.11a Avoid pointless or irrelevant personal information

The head of your company may be the mother of two, the skip of a curling team, a fan of F. Scott Fitzgerald, and a superb cook; none of that is relevant when she announces a stock split. Similarly, identifying a charged criminal as belonging to a particular ethnic group does little to enlighten your readers and may tend to make them draw unfounded generalizations.

8.11b Avoid faint praise

"Women are better than men at routine, repetitious jobs" not only insults men but suggests that women aren't very good at varied and creative work.

8.11c Avoid gender bias

In recent years, gender has come to mean the cultural or social roles assigned to men and women, while sex means the physiological or biological aspects of males and females. Many occupational terms have a male or female suffix because of ancient tradition, not modern reality. Changing chairman to chairperson isn't always adequate, in part because it sounds so self-conscious.

Consider the following alternatives:

actress:	actor (though only some actors are eligible for a best actress award)
alderman:	councillor (unless the term is official)
any man:	anyone, anybody
aviatrix:	flyer, pilot
anchorman/ anchorwoman:	anchor
businessman/ businesswoman:	business person, manager, entrepreneur, merchant
chairman/ chairwoman:	chair, convenor, president
cleaning woman:	cleaner
common man:	average person
countryman:	compatriot, fellow citizen
fireman:	firefighter
fisherman:	fisher (that may sound odd at first, but no one says loggerman or carpenterman)
man a counter:	staff a counter, run a counter
man in the street:	ordinary person
mankind:	humanity, humans, people
man-made:	synthetic, artificial
manpower:	workforce, labor force, staff, personnel
policeman/ policewoman:	police officer, constable, deputy (unless the officer's sex is relevant, as when a woman suspect is improperly searched by a policeman)

salesman/ saleswoman:	sales representative, sales clerk, salesperson
stewardess:	flight attendant
waitress:	server, waiter
workman:	worker, employee

Gender bias can also turn up in singular pronouns:

Anyone who bikes without a helmet will eventually get his head examined.

The generic singular pronoun is supposed to be he, but in practice we often prefer they — as in get their head examined. This of course sounds a little odd; how can you have a plural pronoun and a singular noun?

While it doesn't work all the time, pluralizing the antecedent can solve many such problems: People who bike without helmets will eventually get their heads examined.

8.11d Be careful about sexual orientation

"Gay" and "straight" were originally homosexual slang terms that have become standard usage. It's pointless to regret the loss of "gay" as a synonym for "happy," just as it's pointless to wish that "fond" still meant "foolish." While gay can apply to both men and women, you'll be clearer if you refer to "gay men and women" or to "gays and lesbians."

Be careful with terms that may be semantically loaded: "heterosexism" and "homophobia" are terms that criticize anti-gay attitudes, and you should use them only when you can back them up. Otherwise they're just name-calling, like "fag" and "dyke." Gays may feel free to use such terms about themselves, but outsiders should not — just as your mother can use a pet name for you that no one else dare use.

"Transgendered" may mean either someone who lives as a member of the opposite sex, or someone who has actually changed sex. The latter may also be referred to as a "transsexual."

Don't confuse *sexual orientation* and *sexual preference*. Sexual orientation has to do with whether one prefers people of one's own sex or not. Sexual preference has to do with preferring blonds or particular styles of making love.

8.11e   Be careful with ethnic terms

Be very careful about using terms like ethnic, race, and visible minority. Yorkshire pudding is ethnic food just as kreplachs and papadams are. If you intend to mean a group that's culturally, linguistically, physically different from the majority, you may still be on dangerous ground. Don't forget your readers may be reading your words in Karachi or Kyoto, where you might be the very visible minority.

When you must refer to people by ethnic and racial terms, use the terms they prefer: not Eskimo, but Inuit (singular Inuk); not Negro but African-American or black person. Should you capitalize words like black? Some people do, but White looks odd. Stick to using such terms as adjectives, not nouns, and you can usually stay in the lower case: a native attorney, a black poet.

Some terms, like African, Asian, or Oriental are so broad that they become meaningless. Berbers and Bantus are both Africans; Tamils and Japanese are both Asians; in the age of the Pacific Rim, the Orient is really to the west of most North Americans.

If a term like native seems odd to someone whose ancestors have lived in a country for ten generations, consider aboriginal or indigenous. One Canadian term for Native Indians is First Nations. Where possible, be as specific as possible: Not "a Montana Indian," but "a Montana Blackfoot."

8.11f   Be careful with disabilities

You're generally on safer ground with expressions like a person with a disability instead of a disabled person (which sounds as if the person isn't even conscious!).

When you refer to persons with physical or intellectual disabilities, avoid loaded terms like victim, afflicted with, or suffering from. A child may use a wheelchair; the child should not be confined to the wheelchair. Be careful also to distinguish between disability and impairment (generally caused by accident or genetics) and disease.

In the case of intellectual disability and disease, use terms as accurately as possible. Pop psychology has made psychiatrists of us all, but don't use a term like schizophrenic or bipolar unless you really know what you're talking about. Again, put the term in a prepositional phrase: a person with schizophrenia, or people diagnosed with bipolar disorder.

8.11g   Be careful about age

North Americans are sensitive about their age, which may explain why we like euphemisms: golden ager rather than old person, for example. Only an old person should feel free to use terms like geezer or old fart, and even then it may be more distracting than amusing.

Young people feel patronized by terms like kid or youngster. Up to about the age of 16, they're boys and girls. After that they're men and women, or young persons. If a person's age is important to what you're writing about, mention it:

> John Chang, 19, is already a dot-com millionaire. At 79, Alma Jones is running in her 20th marathon.

If age is irrelevant, don't bother with it.

8.12 Capitalization

Consult a dictionary or one of the style guides mentioned for details on capitalization. What follows deals with some special cases that webwriters should be aware of.

8.12a Capitalize trade names

Someone left a Styrofoam cup and a box of Kleenex on the Xerox copier.

If Valium doesn't work, try a Zoloft. If that doesn't work, take an aspirin; in Canada, you should take an Aspirin.

NOTE: Companies holding trade names often prosecute writers who fail to capitalize them. This is to prevent the trade names from becoming generic and therefore available for anyone to use. This happened with brand names like Nylon, Lanolin, and Cellophane.

Similarly, follow the manufacturer's usage in capitalizing high-tech brand names, even when these include capitals within the word (also known derisively as "StudlyCaps").

WordPerfect

PowerPoint

8.12b SI/Metric units

Only the word Celsius takes a capital in Systéme International/metric terms.

10 km (kilometers)

50 g (grams)

10 ha (hectares)

25 mg (milligrams)

EXCEPTION: SI terms based on proper names take a capital, and so does the abbreviation for liter.

60 V (volts) — from Volta

100 G (gauss) — from Gauss

2 L (liters)

8.12c   Capitalizing lists

If a bulleted list is grammatically part of the sentence that introduces it, listed items do not take capitals.

Chesterton offers you —

> great skiing
>
> superb snowboarding
>
> exciting mountain biking
>
> exhilarating whitewater rafting
>
> awesome rock climbing

If the list is made up of complete sentences, each listed item does take a capital.

Why visit Chesterton?

> It's got great skiing from November to April.
>
> It's got superb snowboarding.
>
> Mountain biking challenges everyone from novices to professionals.
>
> Whitewater rafting is the best in the country.
>
> Rock climbing is awesome, but not for the faint-hearted.

8.12d   Compound words

When a new term, made up of two or more words, comes into the language, we usually write it as separate words — for example, electronic mail, or Web site. But we soon hyphenate it or shorten it, or both. Electronic mail soon became e-mail, and has already become email for many of its users. Web site is still common, but many people prefer website. Web-site is very rare.

While practice does vary on the Web, the following compound-word usages appear to be preferred by most current users:

email

web page

website

webwriter

In many cases, hyphens help to make our meaning clear, and we'd better hang on to them. Consider, for example:

I resent your message.

I re-sent your message.

In the same manner, do we want more advanced research (additional programs like present advanced research), or "more-advanced research " (programs that go beyond what we're doing now)? Was she wearing a "light brown coat" or a "light-brown coat"? Is he an "old computer expert" (aged but technically up to date), or an "old-computer expert" (capable of fixing a Lisa)?

Many compound terms, when they serve as adjectives, take hyphens:

a 50-year-old rock climber

our day-to-day routine

she joined a well-established firm

When we turn such phrases around, we drop the hyphens:

the rock climber is 50 years old

we follow the same routine from day to day

her firm is well established

EXCEPTIONS

When a compound phrase contains an -ly adverb, don't use a hyphen:

an insanely great computer

a truly astounding event

the triumphantly grinning winner

And don't hyphenate a compound containing a comparative or superlative:

She is the least known but most influential editor in the city.

Flash is one of the more dramatic tools for website creation.

8.12e Measurements and numerical terms

Americans are heavy users of the Web, and Americans also use the medieval "imperial" measurement system abandoned by every other civilized nation. The Systéme international d'unités (SI) is the generally accepted version of the metric system. As a webwriter you should be able to supply measurement terms that are meaningful to both Americans and the other six billion people on the planet.

If your Website needs to present measurements, and you expect readers from all over the world, you should display terms in both SI and imperial units.

Imperial and traditional units of measurement

Traditional units can be confusing, especially to international readers. A Canadian gallon, for example, is larger than an American gallon. If you must use traditional measurement units, try to be consistent. Where your readers might need metric equivalents, be sure to supply them. Also, try to avoid mixing metric and traditional units: In Canada, where metric hasn't been fully adopted, people tend to write: "I paid $1.25 a liter for gas, and my car gets only 15 miles per gallon."

Here is a table of some common traditional units of measurement and their metric equivalents. Note that traditional-unit abbreviations usually take periods, while metric abbreviations do not.

Name/Abbreviation	Metric Equivalent
1 pound/lb	.454 g
1 ounce/oz.	.28 g
1 US ton/ton	907 kg
1 imperial ton/ton	1016 kg
1 inch/in.	2.5 cm
1 foot/ft.	0.3 m
1 mile/mi.	1.6 km
1 square foot/sq. ft.	0.09 m2
1 yard/yd.	0.91 m
1 acre/acre	4047 m2
1 acre/acre	0.40 ha (hectares)
1 cubic foot/ft.	0.02 m3
1 US gallon/gal.	3.78 L
1 imperial gallon/gal.	4.54 L
50 degrees Fahrenheit/°F	10°C

8.12f   Numbers in general

In most cases, use words for numbers below 10, and numerals for numbers above 10:

seven days, 14 links, one and only, 11 men to a side

If a number begins a sentence, always spell it out:

Fifteen men sat on a dead man's chest.

Six dollars will get you a ticket.

But if a number is part of an address, a title, a brand, or an organization's name, follow its usage even at the beginning of a sentence:

195 Kinloch Lane was at the end of the street.

7Up is a popular soft drink.

4587 Corporation is a little-known holding company.

When providing two different sets of numbers, use words for one and numerals for the other:

We have 6 two-bedroom suites, 1 studio apartment, and 4 three-bedroom suites.

Use a hyphen when writing out numbers between 21 and 99:

Thirty-nine students crammed the classroom.

One hundred and sixty-two emails arrived overnight.

Don't use commas with long, spelled-out numbers or mixed numbers:

Pay to the order of John Smith: One thousand two hundred fifty-five dollars.

He stands six feet 11 inches tall.

He covered the course in one hour 15 minutes 16 seconds.

SI Numerals

When using SI terms in technical material, use a combination of numerals and abbreviations: 1.6 km, NOT 1.6 kilometres. In other material, use numerals with spelled-out units: Drive 10 kilometres south from the bridge and follow the signs to the vineyard. Do NOT use spelled-out words and SI abbreviations (ten km).

In SI usage, a space replaces the comma in numbers with five or more digits:

50 000 votes

$145 000

The space is optional with four digits:

1 152 votes

1152 votes

If four- and five-digit numbers are mixed, all should have a space:

Our opponents spent $9 000 while we spent $10 500.

SI measurements include some units that aren't really SI, including time. What follows is a list of measurements and their abbreviations, which you should present consistently.

Name	Symbol	Quantity
ampere	A	electric current
bel	B	sound intensity
coulomb	C	electric charge
degree Celsius	ºC	temperature
hectare	ha	area (100 square meters)
hertz	Hz	frequency
Kelvin	K	temperature
kilogram	kg	weight (2.2 pounds)
knot	kn	1,852 meters per hour
liter	L	volume
meter	m	length
minute	'	plane angle
minute	min	time
nautical mile	M	1,852 m (marine distance)
second	"	plane angle
tonne	t	1,000 kg (2,200 pounds)

9. Online Advice about Online Writing Style

Here are some websites that offer good advice about writing for the Web. Such sites usually offer still more links to additional resources. You can also find more resources by using search engines and keying in phrases such as "Web style" or "webwriting" or "writing for the Web."

- Tim Berners-Lee's CERN Style Guide: www.w3.org/Provider/Style/Introduction.html

- Jakob Nielsen: www.useit.com/papers/webwriting

- Yale Center for Advanced Instructional Media Web Style Guide: http://info.med.yale.edu/caim/manual

- Joe Gillespie's Web Page Design for Designers: www.wpdfd.com/wpdhome.htm

- Jeffrey Zeldman's A List Apart: www.alistapart.com

- Web Pages that Suck: http://webpagesthatsuck.com

- CIO Magazine: Content Management: www.cio.com/summaries/web/content

- David Siegel's Net Tips for Writers and Designers (Web Wonk): www.dsiegel.com/tips/index.html

6

CORPORATE WEBWRITING

While the writing principles discussed in this book apply to all websites, writing text for corporate sites is different in some ways than writing for noncorporate sites. A corporate website reflects the consensus of a formal group — a company, a university, a government agency — about how it ought to present itself on the Web.

A commercial website for a retail outlet or webzine, for example, is more likely to reflect a single individual's vision, whether quirky or conformist. A corporate website is the result of a lot of meetings, and the input from a lot of sources may or may not help those who actually put the site together.

Admittedly, a corporate site may also reflect a single person's vision — if that person can sell it to the rest of the group creating the website. But in general, a corporate site is usually a compromise of some kind. If you are the webwriter for such a group, you face a host of largely political challenges in turning those compromises into good writing.

1. Challenges for Corporate Webwriters

Your first challenge as a corporate webwriter is to make your group understand what the Web can and cannot do, and how a website can further the group's interests. If you are also the group's webmaster, you presumably have the technical understanding of the requirements. You accept that part of your job is to educate your group about those requirements, and your group will usually take your word as final.

But it may be harder to explain to them the text requirements of a good site. You can explain how the writing on your group's site can exploit the Web's advantages while avoiding its pitfalls, but it may take a while to make your message understood. Most of us, after all, defer to the HTML guru. But most of us also think that *anyone* can write, so opinions on website content are easy to get.

What if you're not the webmaster, and the group has called you in after accepting the technical suggestions of a non-writer? Then you could have a problem, because the designer may have been concerned with technical questions of display, not with the principles of Orientation, Information, and Action.

As a webwriter you may face yet another tangle: Your group may not have a consensus on what its own interests are and how the site will advance them. Very often, groups automatically adopt the old-fashioned communication model of the FedEx courier, delivering a message against all odds to a passive recipient whose only part in the process is to sign for the package. They aren't thinking about the you attitude discussed in Chapter 2; good webwriting expresses ideas in terms of the reader's advantage. Too often, groups want to go onto the Web to talk only about how wonderful and important they are — not about how they can make themselves useful to their readers.

Marijke Rijsberman, a webwriter for a Silicon Valley consulting firm, puts it this way:

> *The company decides (and lots of companies are deciding the same thing) that [web] content should be taken care of*

in the marketing department, as the gaggle of talent and experience most pertinent to the task. But the thing marketing departments typically do is take care of the message — what we want others to know about the company, whether or not they want to know about the company. The basic mindset is that of advertising: breaking into the awareness of people who are not looking for the information we want them to have.

I suppose the model works for banner ads. But it does not work for other writing on the Web, which needs to recognize that people come looking for you. Of course, they don't come looking for ads, they come on the general assumption that the Web is an information-rich medium that may contain the answers to their questions.

So yes, they may want to know about your company, but chances are that they really want information that's within the company's expertise and they want that information much more than the stuff you put in the corporate brochure.

Web analyst and engineer Jakob Nielsen argues that most corporate websites are not just failures, but are actively damaging to their creators' reputations. While he focuses on commercial sites, I think his findings are equally true for other group-sponsored sites.

The evidence Nielsen offers is pretty devastating. He cites one study of 15 big commercial websites in which users could find information only 42 percent of the time, even though they started from the home page each time. In another study, three out of five online shoppers had given up trying to find the item they wanted to buy. A third survey found that, out of 20 major sites, simple website organization principles (for example, Is the site organized by user goals?) were observed only half the time.

"The odds are against any company that wants to put up a website," says Nielsen. "In my estimate, 90 percent of commercial websites have poor usability."

The problem, Nielsen argues, isn't even confined to "B2C" (business-to-consumer) sites. Well into the Web's second decade, he complains that "Business-to-business (B2B) sites are stuck in the 1990s in their attitude toward the user experience." His current tests show that users achieve only a 58 percent success rate in completing tasks on B2B sites (www.useit.com/alertbox/b2b.html).

This poor success rate is all the more baffling because the decision-makers are usually very focused on pleasing customers in ordinary marketplaces. Imagine a car dealership where you couldn't find a car (or a sales rep) on the lot, or a supermarket where you couldn't find the fresh produce or the checkout stands. Imagine a loan officer who bragged about the bank's assets, but never asked about your own financial needs.

Much of the problem with corporate websites is poor structure: visitors receive inadequate orientation, so they can't navigate to the information they want. And of course, if they don't have the information, they won't perform the action desired of them by the group running the site: to buy the product, to join the party, to apply for admission to the college.

But even when the site design is good, the quality of the writing may make the information unusable and the desired action unappealing to most readers.

2. Define Your Audience

A corporate site should reach a wide range of readers without trying to be all things to all people. A college site should address students (potential and enrolled), faculty, support staff, potential employees, and employers. A bank should address its own staff, its current and potential customers, and the business community. A municipal government site should address its residents and taxpayers, its staff, and potential investors.

All corporate sites should of course address the general public as well, but they will do that best by showing they know how to address their specific audiences.

In some cases, the site may invite particular readers to pages created just for them. Many companies, for example, list "Job Opportunities" as a link on their front page. Pages intended strictly for internal use by staff can be password protected.

Large organizations may be able to afford intensive research into their audiences, which of course will help them focus their website. In any case, it's important that a corporate site express a consistent tone that is appropriate to its intended audiences. (I discuss semantics and register in Chapter 8.) That means achieving a consensus within your organization both about your audience and about the best way to address it.

3. Corporate Webwriting Needs the "You" Attitude

In Chapter 3, I mentioned the FedEx communication model. Until fairly recently, most people — including writers — grew up learning to communicate in school and the workplace using that model, which assumes an active sender and a passive receiver for every message. The message itself is a lump of information that the receiver accepts like a downloaded file. The standard metaphors for this model are either postal ("Get the message?") or ballistic ("We're targeting the 18-to-35 demographic").

The technical term for this model is *instrumental*, because it works on the passive receiver like a crowbar or baseball bat, to create a specific desired response. The implicit message in this model is "Do what I say."

The instrumental FedEx model works fine in media like print, radio, or TV. That's because the receiver has little or no chance to respond beyond a letter to the editor or a phone call to a talk-back line. Communication is effectively one-way.

But as I argued in Chapter 3, the Web really runs on a much more sophisticated constructivist model, in which both sides constantly change roles — sending and receiving at virtually the same time, adapting each message in the light of the last response. Both parties construe the meaning of the exchange, and it may end with both sides in unexpected territory, knowing things they didn't expect to know. The metaphor here is the conversation, and the implicit message is "Is this what you want?"

Even the old FedEx model expects the receiver to sign for the package, or regurgitate the lecture, or vote as the spin doctor wishes. But it's still a vertical relationship between the boss and the bossed. On the Web, relationships are far more horizontal, and anyone who doesn't care to be bossed can escape with the click of a mouse.

And that message, to use a ballistic metaphor, has still not penetrated the thick skulls of many website sponsors — even the organizations that live or die by pleasing their customers and supporters. The message on their sites is pure ego: We do this, we do that, we can make you happy, so make us happy by doing what we want you to do.

The Canadian scholar Northrop Frye once distinguished between *ego art* and *self art*. Ego art sees everyone as a worshipful audience for the ego's own splendor; the only purpose of the audience is to admire the perfect, unchangeable, yet always insecure ego. Self art, by contrast, wants to provoke a response from other selves, to learn and change. The self, being secure, doesn't fear change — or challenge.

In business, good writing requires a "you" attitude that concentrates solely on the customer and the customer's needs. You don't even say: "We have a great deal for you, so do what we say" — you say: "You can take advantage of a great deal, if this is the deal you want." In other words, the constructivist, self-art model is interactive, a conversation with the reader/customer rather than an egomaniac's monologue.

So in the interactive medium of the Web, writers must keep their own egos offstage, and engage the reader on terms of equality and shared interests. The webwriter expects to learn as well as teach, to buy as well as sell — to move and to be moved. Such writing avoids fulsome, manipulative flattery. It sends a nonverbal message of respect and interest. A site that's slow to load and hard to navigate is an ego site. A quick-loading site with good navigation reflects a self site, considerate of readers. Webtext that's precious or bombastic may say a lot about the writer's big vocabulary, but it speaks much more loudly of the writer's big ego.

Even if we grew up as writers in the FedEx world of print on paper, we need to recognize that the old model doesn't work here. Our readers may not know instrumentalism from constructivism, but they know when they're getting respect and when they're not. On the Web they enjoy a power of response that we ignore at our peril. But if we remember the you attitude and engage them in a genuine dialogue (as *The Cluetrain Manifesto* argues we should), we will all profit from every online conversation.

 You can read *The Cluetrain Manifesto: The End of Business as Usual* at www.cluetrain.com. It's a thought-provoking challenge to everyone who wants to make money on the Web.

4. Too Many Webwriters Can Spoil the Site

Bureaucracies, whether corporate or governmental, can make life hard for the webwriter. Web designer Stephen Martin has seen what can happen when an organization allows too many people to do their own thing on its website:

> *In the government world (and on many of the private sector sites I've worked on), the sites sometimes get compartmentalized by the group or department responsible for that area of the business (e.g., the Office of Management and Budget is responsible for the management and budget pages of the website). This often leads to a highly inconsistent site because there are so many different levels of experience and expertise working on the site. I've found that people also get very defensive about their writing (it's the "everyone's a*

writer" syndrome). They tend to write in long-winded flowery prose, or they are so terse as to be incoherent to all but those who are intimately familiar with the subject.

The writing process is also subject to so many levels of approval that what you end up with looks nothing like what you started with. Imagine if everything you wrote went through a review by at least 12 different people (90 percent of whom are not writers or editors by trade).

Trying to set guidelines and standards for content (even very broad standards) often leads to a backlash since different agencies and departments are very territorial and not about to give up what they see as their right to control "their section of the site." Most view my group more as an Internet service provider than as the site's administrators and developers.

In other words, writing for a government website is often an exercise in futility.

While Martin's view reflects a real situation, don't let it discourage you. If you are writing for a corporate website, private or public, you may need to be a very good politician and a patient advocate. When you make your case for good, consistent writing on the site, follow the three webwriting principles mentioned in Chapter 2:

- Give your group the orientation it needs about the Web.

- Give it information it can use.

- Give it reasons to act in what it clearly understands are its own best interests.

Whether they're marketing government statistics, college courses, party memberships, or shareware, your colleagues need to understand how marketing works on the Web — and you're the person who has to sell them on that concept.

This doesn't mean sermonizing to these groups during committee meetings. More likely it will mean presenting them with a basic concept and approach toward the creation of the website that they can understand, that harmonizes with the group's communication style in other media, and that gives them the kind of jolt that visitors to the site should get.

Critical to the success of a corporate website is a clear, consistent style guide. You may have many contributors to your site's text, and their varied voices may help to attract and hold visitors. But in matters of usage, vocabulary, and display, your text should be clear, concise, and correct.

5. Components of Corporate Websites

Depending on the kind of organization, your website may have few or many components. But they will all fit into the orientation/ information/action pattern.

Orientation will tell your visitors where they are and what your corporate purpose is. This includes the About Us page, which may include organization history, policies, and ways of contacting the organization. Even here, the "you" attitude is important. You're talking about yourself, but in terms that show readers how you can provide what they're looking for.

One element in the orientation component needs some special attention: the mission statement.

5.1 Mission statements

Placing a mission statement on a website may pose a challenge to webwriters. Nancy Eaton, editor of the webzine *Retro*, warns against "passive voice, formal tone, hype," and other language abuses; mission statements are all too often rich in examples of such abuses. What's more, using an overly formal tone or passive voice may mean your mission statement does not accurately represent your organization.

So if you're going to put your organization's mission statement on your site (and you should), maybe you'd better hold a few meetings to examine it first. A good principle for expressing a mission state-ment is WISIWYG — What I Say Is What You Get.

In other words, if you can't deliver it, don't promise it in your mission statement or anywhere else on your site. And if all you promise is jargon and hype, your readers will see that and surf on to a more welcoming site.

Your mission statement should be on a page of its own, with links to other important pages on the site. You can give readers a chance to respond to the statement by including an email link on the mission-statement page — but make it a link to the company president or the chair of the board of directors, not to the company webmaster. That way, readers will understand that their opinions are going straight to the decision-makers.

The information component of a corporate website can break down into many different sections, depending on the organization and its audience. But most sites are likely to offer such sections as Policies, Products, Services, Departments, News, Contacts, Special Users, Archives, and "Good News Surprises."

5.2 Policies

Corporate policies can also pose problems on websites. Many organizations deal with the public under the terms of very specific policies (sometimes self-created, sometimes imposed by law). They tend to take those policies for granted, as the "fine print" that no one pays attention to.

Pay attention to your group's policies. If you're a retailer with an ironclad need for a returned-goods policy that won't bankrupt you, make sure that policy is up on your website, in large print, so you can refer your customers to it if they haven't found it on their own. If you are creating the website for a school board with a spe-cific policy about handling parent complaints, that policy should be up in plain English on your school district's site.

Your group's policies are, in a sense, a contract with the people you serve. Your customers need to know how best to deal with you, and you need to define exactly what you can and can't do for them. And you have to define this in terms that appeal to the reader's own self-interest. It's not an easy job, but do it right and you will enjoy better interaction with your customers.

5.3 Products

Text for products requires careful tailoring for the intended customer. If you're selling a highly technical product to technically sophisticated buyers, you can and should use technical language. It's part of the exformation you share with your customers, and helps to form a bond with them.

But if your customers are non-technical, and just want a product to achieve some desired result, stash the tech details behind a link to a Specifications page. The product text should deal with quality, efficiency, price, ease of use, peace of mind — whatever your market research has taught you about your customers' desires.

5.4 Services

This can be a catch-all, and "services" may vary depending on the organization. At Home Hardware (www.homehardware.ca), a Canadian chain, the "Services" link takes customers to financial services, including gift cards and credit cards. But the home page also offers services under "Projects" and "Helpful Advice" links. For a business catering to do-it-yourselfers, this is smart phrasing.

5.5 Departments

In an organization of any size, reaching the department you want can be a navigation challenge. Columbia University (www.columbia.edu) handles this well with a list of departmental links down the left-hand side of the home page: Academic Programs, Prospective Students, and so on. It also includes an A-Z Index.

Significantly, Columbia's page for potential international students (www.columbia.edu/cu/isso/admit) is written in demanding English. The first paragraph scores at 13.2 with the Kincaid formula (fairly hard), and 35.4 on the Flesch index (also fairly hard). This sends a nonverbal message about the level of English fluency expected of international students. Perhaps in this case, short words and short sentences would not serve readers well.

5.6 News

When your organization sends out news releases, they should certainly appear on your own website as well. While they can follow the standard organization and tone of a news story (Who, What, When, Where, Why, and How), you can exploit the interactivity of the web. If the release is about a report you've published, the release can link to the report, as with the Canadian Centre for Policy Alternative's release "Five tests for Canada's next federal budget" (www.policyalternatives.ca/news/2009/01/pressrelease2080/?pa=BB73645).

If news is important enough to warrant its own department or page, then updates should be frequent. When the latest news story on your site is six months old, that's news too — bad news for your organization.

5.7 Archives

You don't have to persuade your group to abandon everything it knows about communicating with the public through other media. Much of your site's content can be plain old print text stored on your site in the form of archives.

Annual and special reports, news releases, and texts of executives' speeches can all go straight into your site's archives, whether as text files or as PDF (portable document format) files that retain their original word-processed format. You may be able to add value to these archives by creating links within the text to other resources on your site or on the Web, but even as simple archives, such documents are a valuable service to your readers.

Other documents may work either as straight archives or as hypertext. For example, a collective agreement could appear as a straight scrolling text, or as a sequence of chunks, each just a few paragraphs long. Links on such short pages could show readers how one part of the agreement influences another. Policies can be organized similarly, perhaps with links to relevant laws or to comparable policies in other organizations.

5.8 "Good news surprises"

Whether you're running an advocacy organization or a profit-making business, a key aspect of gaining support is the good news surprise: Offering your visitors something agreeable that they didn't expect. It might be a free offer, or access to information they didn't expect to find, or an opportunity to do something they didn't think you could do. This kind of good news is a welcome jolt that can build good will and attract return visits.

5.9 Action items

Corporate websites are more than just online newsstands. They exist to inspire action in their visitors, and the desired action should be clearly visible on the home page: Email us, subscribe to our free newsletter, donate to our cause, join our forum. The Barack Obama website (www.barackobama.com) invites many kinds of action, from buying a mug or t-shirt to joining a Facebook group. Given that the site was clearly important in winning the presidency, not to mention raising hundreds of millions of dollars, BarackObama.com deserves careful attention from webwriters.

Exercise 7: Critiquing Corporate Websites

Visit a number of corporate websites, including a big-box retailer, a major technology corporation, and an international nongovernmental organization. Which, in your opinion, is most effective in orientation, information, and action?

7

WRITING FOR BLOGS

The emergence of the web log, or blog for short, has been one of the most important developments in the history of the Internet. In the 1990s, blogs were the domain of technically skilled persons who knew HTML very well. It was easy for them to design a site and then update it whenever they liked. The rest of us, struggling with early authoring tools like Globetrotter and FrontPage, were glad just to get a page of content up, with functioning links.

So the original blogs tended to reflect their authors' technical interests. As they rummaged around on the early Web, they found sites that interested them and created links to them. That made their own sites more interesting to others sharing the same interest.

As more people became comfortable with web authoring, blogs began to multiply. They also became more personal. New applications emerged that enabled bloggers to create professional-looking sites without knowing much HTML at all.

Blog topics multiplied. By the turn of the century, bloggers were offering the world their opinions on politics, knitting, movies, and every other subject. By the time I got into blogging in 2003, some basic conventions and genres had emerged. As we approach the end of the decade, blogs continue to evolve, sometimes in surprising directions.

1. Personal Blogs

The vast majority of blogs are the expressions of individuals or small groups concerned with personal matters. They divide into introvert and extrovert blogs.

The introvert blog is all about the author's private life: joys and sorrows, intimate relationships, daily events, and so on. These may touch on larger issues, but only in passing.

One of the striking aspects of this genre is the author's self-criticism: The blog is purported to be "chaos," "random," "neurotic," and generally reflective of a failed life.

The content bears this out; posts are often highly self-critical, describing work not done, tests flunked, relationships failed. Even long gaps in the blogging record require mention and apology. Against this background, occasional highlights appear: a wonderful concert attended, a happy dinner with family, a new job. No need to single out any examples; they're all over the blogosphere.

The audience for such blogs consists, I'd guess, of the author and a small number of friends, who will sometimes post encouraging responses.

But introvert blogs now include some dramatic and powerful sites whose authors are battling serious diseases or disabilities. At "ldfc," (www.ldfc.co.il) for example, the Israeli blogger Lior Dangoor describes his experiences with cancer since it was diagnosed in 2007. "I'm Fighting Cancer" (www.imfightingcancer.com) describes an anonymous blogger's efforts to find out if his symptoms mean prostate cancer.

Such blogs are far from the self-absorbed; their real function is to share experience and give support to others. The quality of their writing is generally very good.

Another kind of personal record is in the extrovert blog, in which the author pays more attention to the surroundings. A great example is Big White Guy in Hong Kong (http://bigwhiteguy.com), a Canadian expat's funny and opinionated view of life in his adopted city.

2. Job Blogs

Another genre is the job blog, in which the focus is on events at work. Depending on your interest in the job, this can be boring or fascinating. It's also a genre that has evolved very rapidly into several subgenres.

One of my favorites job blogs is Oh Jen Jen's It's a Zoo Out There (www.spacefan.blogspot.com). She's a medical officer at Changi General Hospital in Singapore. In the spring of 2003 her blog was a mesmerizing narrative of the hospital's struggle to contain SARS — a struggle that cost the lives of several admired colleagues.

Dr. Oh's blog is clearly aimed at her colleagues, but during the height of the SARS outbreak she was being read around the world. Now she's back to routine emergency-room problems and talking about her favorite TV programs.

A hazard of the job blog, of course, is that it can cost you your job if you're indiscreet or your employers would prefer you not to talk in public about anything related to your work.

But some job blogs are actually written by the chief executive officer, and they can be very powerful marketing tools. Consider Jim Hiller, CEO of Hiller's Markets in Michigan (www.hillers.com/blog). When he explains why his stores don't sell cigarettes, or why he drives American cars, he builds a personal bond with his customers. They may not agree with him, but chances are that even smokers and Honda drivers will keep shopping at his stores.

Some business leaders hate the idea of running their own blogs. They rightly suspect it will add to their workload, and they fear they'll say something that gets them and their firm into trouble. But CEO blogging is such a big field that it even has its own blog support, like "Business Blog Advice," (http://www.ceoblogwatch.com).

CEO blogs are also a feature of corporate intranets, enabling boss and staff to maintain a close relationship. In naming the "10 Best Intranets of 2009," (www.useit.com/alertbox/intranet_design.html), Jakob Nielsen noted that such intranets usually feature a CEO blog.

Workspace blogs have become a convenient way for some people to do a job and to record the results. Rather than build folders full of bookmarks to sites they use on the job, they put the links onto a blog. Their posts may be documents they've created using such links, or simply a diary of work done. In 2007 I created such a workspace blog when I embarked on a major revision of a book first published in 1978. As I discovered online resources, I added the links. It became a very comfortable way to produce a 60,000-word manuscript requiring a great many changes from the original.

While my workspace blog was a one-person job, such blogs can also work for teams whose members all contribute something to the final product. They can be public, or password-protected. In a private blog, the writing can be messy or precise, depending on the bloggers' preferences. Only when the material created is to become public do the bloggers need to worry about style, usage, and text display.

Course blogs can be a useful form of workspace blog, but not in ways that you might think. For years I created a blog for each of the college courses I was teaching. It would include relevant links (such as tourism sites for tourism students). I could post course materials, supplementary items, and news updates, and I hoped such sites would enhance the value of the course for the students.

Such was not the case. Overwhelmed with work, the students tended to avoid what seemed like just another chore. Even when I made students co-authors, they rarely posted. Perhaps I could have coerced them into participating by making blog participation part of their grade, but that seemed to me to undercut the real value of online learning: to go where you want to go and learn what matters to you.

What's more, course blogs turned out to be much more work for me. I had to keep uploading class handouts so that students who'd missed class would be able to download them. In effect, I was making it easier for students to cut class.

However, I did find one real use for course blogs: They're far better than PowerPoint as lecture platforms. I could upload handouts and print them out as well. Since my classes were all in rooms with networked teaching stations and projectors, I could simply go online, log in to the blog, and go through the material. While students would have a hard copy of each handout, I could also project it on the screen and walk them through it.

In many cases, the course blog would contain links to directly relevant materials, which I could use for lecture or discussion purposes. In an advanced tourism course, the students were working as "consultants" for real businesses; we could visit our clients' websites, critique them, and discuss ways to improve them. The course blog for my film students was also useful, since I could link to sites with video clips. Discussing propaganda techniques in film, we could look at everything from Nazi posters to clips of North Korea's Kim Jong Il riding a white horse to will.i.am's "Yes We Can" video.

In this respect, course blogs are very convenient for all kinds of presentations, and I've continued to use them for webwriting workshops, such as the one I gave for the Manitoba Association for Distance Learning and Training (http://crofsblogs.typepad.com/madlat).

3. Specialist Blogs

The specialist blog can be a variant of the job blog, but the specialty may be just one aspect of the job, or a hobby. The specialist is clearly speaking to colleagues, comfortable with a technical vocabulary that may baffle outsiders. Emphasis here is often more on the audience than on the author, with plenty of links to other specialist sites.

Here the blogger is providing both new and old resources to a "community of interest." The community may be those interested in the career of some movie star, or new findings in archaeology, or the minute-by-minute progress of a World Cup soccer game.

The specialist blogger assumes most readers are familiar with the shop talk of the specialty, whether it's soccer or circuit design. This raises a writing problem: Should the writer avoid technical terms, or stop to explain them? Other specialists will be annoyed at constant interruptions to define what they already know. Newcomers to the field will be baffled by the jargon.

One possible compromise is to turn technical terms into links that take the reader to a glossary (or to create definitions that pop up when the reader's cursor rolls over such terms).

Almost by accident, I created a specialist blog based on my experience teaching standard English grammar and usage. "Ask the English Teacher" (http://crofsblogs.typepad.com/english) gets over 500 visitors a day even though I rarely update it. But if you want to know the difference between "drink, drank, and drunk," Google will take you there.

Another of my specialist blogs, "Writing Fiction," (http://crofsblogs.typepad.com/fiction), was intended to be a journal about the writing of a new science-fiction novel. But I also used it as an archive of materials I'd developed for a fiction-writing course, and posted occasional items of interest to aspiring writers. The course materials then turned into a stand-alone, do-it-yourself online course, "Write a Novel," (http://crofsblogs.typepad.com/novel), which includes suggested exercises to help writers solve problems in dialogue, plot, and so on.

While I still don't know much about bird flu, I've learned a great deal about organizing information on a website, making it useful for everyone from journalists and scientists to ordinary people trying to learn about the subject.

Book blogs are another form of specialization: online supplements to print books. My workspace blog Pioneers (http://crofsblogs.typepad.com/pioneers) is now a book blog, used for promoting and updating the new edition of my book.

Similarly, this book has a blog, Writing for the Web (http://crofsblogs.typepad.com), where the online index and references are available. The previous edition of this book came with a CD in every copy, but this turned out to be less useful than we'd expected. Mac users found the CD was unreadable, so I uploaded its links and resources as a simple Word file readable to any computer. As well, students using that edition as a textbook found they couldn't upload it to university computers programmed to be hostile to strange CDs.

The book blog, therefore, is a good solution for providing extra value online, as well as providing a forum where book users can keep up with the subject and offer their own views and experiences.

4. News Blogs

A news blog may be part of the online service of a print newspaper or a broadcaster's website. As such, it can both update news reports and create an archive for them. During the 2006 World Cup, many newspapers blogged the games, minute by minute. At the same time, they were running other blogs on their sites to cover news about technology, entertainment, business issues, travel, and education.

Some individuals and groups run news blogs as a way of putting scattered information in one place: World Cup coverage, for example (www.worldcupblog.org). Daily New Zealand News (http://newszealand.blogspot.com) summarizes events in New Zealand. And eMercedesBenz (www.emercedesbenz.com) reports news about Mercedes-Benz cars.

But you don't have to be a full-time professional journalist to run a news blog. My own site H5N1 (http://crofsblogs.typepad .com/h5n1) gathers news about avian flu, and draws visitors from around the world.

This was originally a "self-educational" blog: In 2005 I realized I didn't know anything about avian flu, and built the blog as a place to store what I was learning. Since then, H5N1 has become a component of "Flublogia," an online community of interest stretching around the world.

I try to keep the text of H5N1 as short and clear as possible; many of my readers would be lost if I didn't. While I often analyze or comment on the stories I post, I prefer to let the stories speak for themselves, and to let readers draw their own conclusions. (When I'm excerpting technical reports, I usually stick to the abstract — and I break it up into short paragraphs.)

The line between news and advocacy can often blur. You may link only to stories that support your view of the world, or your own comments on those stories may contain a strong bias. Your readers will always know where you stand, but they may also find you predictable and therefore not worth many repeat visits.

5. Advocacy Blogs

In an advocacy blog, the blogger is arguing the case for a group, movement, or philosophy: to promote Partners in Health (www.pih.org/index.html), or strongly conservative American politics (www.littlegreenfootballs.com/weblog/weblog.php). Most corporate blogs are advocates for their organizations.

Some political advocacy blogs, especially in the United States, enjoy huge readerships and make money through the sale of online ads. If you dream of running a big, popular advocacy blog, do a very careful analysis of sites like InstaPundit (http://instapundit.com) or Daily Kos (www.dailykos.com). As well as studying the design, test the readability of the text on such sites.

You may find that, in some ways, advocacy blogs seem exempt from the rules this book proposes. Consider, for example, Glenn Greenwald's "Unclaimed Territory" blog at Salon.com (www.salon.com/opinion/greenwald).

While Greenwald uses a readable serif font and runs his text in a narrow column, he also writes long paragraphs full of long sentences. He quotes long passages, putting them in hard-to-read italics, and sometimes he even boldfaces the italics. Greenwald's posts are also usually very long, and readers have to scroll right through them rather than jump to another page.

Yet his column is extremely popular and influential. It seems that when the content is important to readers, they'll put up with layout and text display that should drive them away.

Greenwald's blog dramatizes an old story in advertising: An ad man once told a friend named Max that he could make him read a full newspaper page of 8-point type. The secret: "The headline would be, 'This page is all about Max.'" Greenwald's liberalism and legal philosophy are evidently all about his readers. They share his exformation about American politics.

By the same token, advocacy blogs can have terrible text display, clumsy writing, and even spelling and grammar errors — as long as they strengthen their core readers' opinions and values. Those same drawbacks will only give extra reasons for unbelievers to reject such advocates. (For more discussion of advocacy principles, see Chapter 8.)

Collective blogs can often provide more information than any single individual can, and they're increasingly popular with advocacy sites and news gatherers. My own experience with The Hook (http://thetyee.ca/Blogs/TheHook), the politics blog of the online magazine *The Tyee*, has taught me that a collective blog can cover a remarkable range of topics, in different styles, and still retain a distinct identity.

For writers on such blogs, the major problems are administrative. For example, who's going to blog about a given news story? How many stories should go up per day, or per hour? Are we blogging about hard news, or offering mostly opinion? Do we as a collective, have a "position"?

Whatever the decisions, the collective should try to maintain reasonably consistent usage and a style with which most of its readers are comfortable.

Whatever the genre, much of the writing in the blog world is pretty bad. But I hope and believe that it will improve as bloggers become more comfortable with the medium and with the conventions of their preferred genres. Bloggers will try to emulate the writers they admire, and to distance themselves from the bad writers. In science fiction, Sturgeon's Law decrees that "90 percent of everything is crud." We can strive to reduce blog junk to a somewhat smaller percentage.

6. Developing the Right Style for Your Blog

Of course these categories often overlap. A news blog may be specialized, like World Cup Blog. It may include personal comments and social observations, and may strongly advocate a particular agenda. Still, the genres tend to stand apart from one another, and to appeal to very distinct audiences.

The distinctions lie in part in the resources they offer. An introvert blog may link to sites selling the blogger's favorite CDs and books, or to the blogs of friends. An extrovert blog may link to such items, but will also link to governments, advocacy sites, or specialty sites related to the blogger's hobbies and recreations.

Each of these blog genres poses particular writing challenges. Introverts tend to write long paragraphs with very little "you" attitude. Extroverts may lack a consistent focus. Specialists may be so specialized, and so fond of technical shop talk, that they exclude casual visitors.

Advocacy blogs are especially challenging for their writers. As noted earlier, text on a computer screen works best with blunt assertions, not with long, careful arguments. This tends to encourage jolt-rich rhetoric, full of strong language and weak reasoning.

Advocacy bloggers will therefore find themselves talking mostly to the converted, with reference to adversaries only as a pretext for more strong language to jolt the converts.

Maybe some of the most introverted bloggers aren't interested in gaining more traffic, but everyone else is. Readers go to sites that they trust to give them accurate, reliable and current information. Both style and content can help to build that trust, and therefore to build traffic. The three principles of webwriting are helpful.

6.1 Orientation: What your blog is about

Orientation can include:

- Title (avoid obscure or heavily ironic terms)

- Catchphrase (the "subtitle" that helps explain the blog's purpose)

- Main links ("About me," "Email me," and links with obvious relevance to the blog's main topic)

So if you're running a community news blog, your title and catchphrase might be:

Chesterton Newsletter

People, events, and issues in the Chesterton Valley

Consider how your readers might respond if instead you gave your blog a title and catchphrase like:

Chesterton: The Land That Time Forgot

Fighting the Neanderthals on District Council

Your main links are important too. If your profile or "About Me" page is badly written, sarcastic, or simply uninformative, you can't expect readers' trust. If the links to other sites are obviously one-sided, readers will be skeptical: a link to the Communist Party of Canada, but not to the Chesterton municipal website, will not build confidence in your reliability.

Titles and catchphrases can also build traffic-another reason for simple, straightforward titles and catchphrases. If your blog followed the second example, you'd attract people Googling for information about Neanderthals, or the Edgar Rice Burroughs novel *The Land That Time Forgot*. Neither group will care about your local political battles.

When I started my avian-flu blog, I chose H5N1 as the title and gave it a simple catchphrase: "News and resources about avian flu." Within a very few months, I discovered that a Google search for "H5N1" would put my site in the first three or four hits out of millions.

I suggest, then, that you choose your blog's title and catchphrase using clarity, brevity, and terms that your potential readers will type into Google when they want the kind of information you offer.

6.2 Information: What you want to tell your readers

The basic unit of blog prose is not the sentence or the paragraph, but the whole post. In effect, a post is like a miniature web page, usually with chunks of text and links to other sites. And like a web page, it should be able to stand on its own without reference to other pages. (Since blogs usually add new posts at the top, you can't even assume that your readers have seen your earlier posts.)

Each post, then, is a kind of chunk: a mini-essay. As such, it needs structure: an attention-grabbing hook, a clear exposition of your topic, perhaps a glimpse of something not obvious, and a closing "kicker" that wraps up the post.

As with most text to be read online, your posts should be short: short sentences, short paragraphs. When your content requires long, complex presentation, put it into a PDF or word-processed file — or into a video or podcast file.

If you're writing a personal blog for three friends, your style isn't important. You can ignore grammar, punctuation, and spelling — even coherence. Your friends will have the exformation to know what you're talking about. In other blogs, however, lapses from Standard English and routine typos will hurt your credibility.

But speed is the essence of blogging: You can say something quickly, and editing only slows you down. Who has time to write, print out, proofread, correct, and finally post something?

Blogging software itself can help. Most applications can supply at least spell checking. But you can do more than that.

For example, you may miss a typo or spelling error when you're composing. But as soon as you upload your post, the goof jumps out at you — just as if you were proofreading on paper. The change in format seems to make your text unfamiliar, so the errors are easy to spot. Then it's easy to go back, correct the error, and re-post it.

You may also be able to compose a post as a draft, let it cool off, and then return to proofread it before posting. Writing in "draft" format also enables you to create a post, dig up some elusive fact, and then add the fact quickly before posting. If some reader spots an error you've missed, you can easily correct it.

6.3 Action: What you want your readers to do

Depending on the genre of your blog, you may want very little response from your readers, or a lot. A personal blog post invites comments or email from friends. A job blog or advocacy blog may invite readers to take all kinds of action: visit other sites, download documents, sign up for email lists or online forums, or join a professional association or political party.

Most of these actions require links. Some can appear in the post, or at the end of the post. Others can appear in lists displayed in columns alongside your posts. Remember that many readers are hesitant to click through to a site unless the link title, or its blurb, gives them a reason to.

Of course links can also include downloadable materials: PDFs, photos, podcasts and other audio files, and video clips. These can pose problems: the file is too big, or it requires a particular application. If that might pose a problem for some of your readers, you can also include a link to a site where the application is available.

Bloggers usually welcome comments, but this function has hazards. Some comments may be abusive or even defamatory. Others can be "comment spam," planted to attract your visitors to pornography or gambling sites.

Blog applications like TypePad can protect your site by enabling you to delete unwelcome comments. You can even ban all comments from a given Internet Protocol (IP) address. (TypePad can also send you an email message whenever a comment appears on your site, so you can delete comments within minutes of their appearance.)

Keeping your blog free of nuisances can be time-consuming, but it's the price you pay for an interactive site — and if your site isn't interactive, it's just electronic graffiti.

Exercise 9: Reviewing Blogs

Find three roughly comparable blogs — CEO blogs, news blogs, personal blogs — and write a short review of them. Explain what you like and dislike about each site's orientation, information, and action. Do the bloggers' writing styles appeal to you regardless of the site design and text display?

Choose a text-heavy site like Glenn Greenwald's (www.salon.com/opinion/greenwald) and paste the URL into the window at Readability.info (http://readability.info). Note the reading level, sentence length, and other aspects of the text. Do you like the content regardless, or does the analysis help to explain why you don't like the content?

---

7. Online Résumés

When the world economy started falling apart in the summer and fall of 2008, many of us followed the story online through mainstream media websites and countless blogs. And as many of us started to wonder about the safety of our jobs and pensions, it seemed natural to market ourselves online. It could be the most important webwriting we ever compose.

Clearly, your online résumé should make you appear useful to potential employers. But if your résumé is going to stand out, you'll need to do things better than most people.

7.1 Make a good first impression

When we write web documents, we bring some habits from print. They don't always apply in hypertext, however, and this is especially true of the résumé.

The print-on-paper résumé works on the principle of the good first impression. First we like (or dislike) the general look of the résumé. Then we gain our impression of the person from the first things we learn about him or her — from what's at the top of the résumé. We carry on through the résumé paying most attention to whatever section comes first, and to whatever is at the top of a given section.

If you put your education at the top of the résumé, we assume that your education is your strongest selling point. If you put your most recent education at the top of the section, we assume that's your most relevant training.

That's why print résumés work in reverse chronological order: they're trying to show employers that the applicant has strong, recent experience or training in areas that the employer thinks are important.

If you follow this principle too closely, of course, you may run into trouble. Suppose you want a job as a tour guide, and you have lots of experience, but since last summer you've kept yourself alive with a series of joe jobs in the local mall. In strict reverse chronology, your work-experience section makes you look like a qualified salesperson, not a tour guide.

The answer in a print résumé is to create a special category, Tour Guide Experience, and another category for the mall jobs,

Other Experience (details available on request), which you put far down the résumé where it won't draw much attention.

So if you're using the Web to market yourself, how do you organize your electronic résumé?

You have a couple of options. You could make it a long, scrolling document, or a stack of short pages linked to a front page. The scrolling document is technically easier to create, since it's just one file and it keeps everything unified. When your readers open your résumé, the first thing they see is whatever you think is your strongest qualification. They can then scroll down through the rest of the résumé, learning more about you. (An excellent guide to creating such a résumé on a blog is available as a tutorial from TypePad: www.typepad.com/tips/professional-tutorial.html.)

If you create a stack of pages, the front page is really just a table of contents, a set of buttons that link to an education page or a work-experience page. This gives your readers the chance to decide for themselves what's most important about you from their point of view: your recent training, your work experience, or your specific work skills.

An alternative could be to create a set of links at the top of a single page: education, tour guide experience, volunteer experience, work skills. The employer can then rappel down your page, hopping straight to the section of most interest — with a button in each section that will lead back to the top of the page for another hop.

Choose the organizational structure you think will create the least trouble for employers. Within each section, display your information as you would in a regular print résumé: for example, job title, summary of duties, perhaps the name of your supervisor and your reason for leaving.

Your school and previous employers have websites — do you provide links? If you do, you're probably wiser putting such links on a separate page or at the bottom of the résumé. Otherwise you risk distracting your readers by inviting them to jump to a site that's really not relevant to your purposes. This résumé is about you, after all, not about your last employer or the college you attended 12 years ago.

7.2 Surprise: Redefine yourself as different

One hazard for all job seekers is presenting the right mix of reassurance and surprise to potential employers. Employers are anxious souls, always worrying that they'll hire the wrong person. That's one reason why they like to see a very traditionally designed résumé; the design itself says you're a traditional, reliable kind of person. Of course, when everyone's doing traditional design, you look like everyone else and the employer may recover from anxiety only to find you boring.

In print, you can set yourself apart from the herd by presenting an unusual layout, by adopting a different tone (maybe very informal), or even by using a distinctive font or pale-lavender paper. On the Web you can do the same things, but they may backfire. Unusual layouts may just look awkward on your employer's particular browser and platform. A page designed for a big monitor may look terrible on a small one. A knockout special effect (or even access to the page itself) doesn't even happen if the reader lacks a particular plug-in. The background color you chose so carefully may never show up if the reader's browser has the wrong settings, and your classy font may not show up either if your reader doesn't have the font on his or her computer.

You will notice that I've discussed only problems with display; on the Web, the reader largely decides how a page will display. But whether your text appears in 12-point Times Roman or 14-point Palatino, the content will remain the same. So it's in content that you'll be able to set yourself apart from your competitors by giving the employer a pleasant surprise or two.

Plain English will be the first such surprise. Many job-seekers on the Web are technical and scientific workers, businesspeople, and bureaucrats. They're used to writing a thick, verbose English even though they say they hate such a style in their colleagues' writing. Where such a technical style is critical to accuracy, it's perfectly OK to use it — but don't use a technical style when you don't need to.

Plain English gives you several advantages in presenting your qualifications in a Web-based résumé:

- Pleasure. Readers can actually understand, at once, what you're telling them. Most will find this a welcome change, and since good writers of plain English are scarce, you've added yet another qualification to your skill list.

- Speed. Remember that the monitor slows down reading speed. Plain English, concisely written, will help readers get the message faster.

- Nonverbal confidence message. Plain English tells the reader you're confident in yourself and your understanding of the field in which you work. You're not trying to impress by using business English or bureaucratese or technobabble.

Sure, you know those dialects, and you can use them when necessary, but you're not talking shop in your résumé — you're making a sales pitch for yourself. The more people who understand you, the more potential employers you have.

Your résumé has other nonverbal messages. These messages are critical for the way they support or undercut your verbal message.

Suppose you're presenting yourself in your text as a capable website designer — but your own site organization is clumsy and confusing, with unappealing graphics and spelling errors in the text. Which message will your readers believe, the verbal (what you say on your site) or the nonverbal (how you say it)? The nonverbal, of course. If you need more proof, look at almost any website designer's page and ask yourself: Would I hire this person to design my own page?

Or suppose you create an exquisitely advanced site, full of clever technical surprises in graphics, audio, and video. The nonverbal message in such a site is: Only the equally technologically advanced, those with all the plug-ins and a really fast Internet connection, need to visit here. That may make some employers feel right at home. Or it may not. The most sophisticated web users understand that you don't do something just because it's technically doable, but rather because it's the simplest, most effective way to convey a message. When such sophisticated users are the kind of employers you want to reach, less really is more.

Probably the best surprise you can offer a potential employer is the nonverbal message that you know your area of expertise, you enjoy using that expertise, and you're not trying to impress anyone with irrelevant information. If you judge your online résumé by the three principles of good webwriting (Orientation, Information, and Action), and it passes, chances are your potential employer will be very pleasantly surprised indeed.

7.3 Create a portfolio on your site

Many job seekers turn up for a hiring interview with a portfolio that demonstrates their skills: reports written for previous employers, copies of ads they've written or designed, photos they've taken, letters of commendation, and awards. These can be an effective way of showing, not just telling, potential employers what you can do for them.

Your website can serve as a portfolio that employers can consult even before they call you in for an interview. Consider some of the items you could include in your portfolio:

- Reference letters

- Awards

- Evaluations by previous employers

- Degrees and certificates

- Course descriptions or outlines (both for courses you've taken and courses you've taught)

- Writing samples: technical reports, business plans, proposals, ad copy, news releases, novels in progress, poetry

- Graphics samples: photos, video clips, line art

- News stories (whether by you or about you)

- Links to organizations or individuals

Some of these elements need careful thought. For example, do you really need to include a scanned graphic of your college degree, or of an award you won as a freelance writer? Are the writing samples really relevant to the job you're seeking, or just the kind of thing you enjoy doing for yourself?

If you provide an email link to a reference or previous employer, has that person given you permission to do so? After all, you're asking the person to go to the trouble of replying to queries about you — maybe a lot of them — and it's simple courtesy to check first to see if that's okay.

7.4 Provide useful services

Your web résumé should supply a benefit — a good-news surprise — to potential employers even if they don't hire you. Maybe you're an accountant who's helped design a new spreadsheet; let your readers link to a demo version of the spreadsheet. Or, as a safety consultant, you developed emergency procedures for open-pit mines; archive your guidelines in easily downloadable form. You were a cook in a local steakhouse? Give us a great barbecue sauce recipe. (In all these examples, I assume you own the rights to what you're offering!)

If you've got the skills to be worth hiring, you know something useful that you can give away. By doing so you build goodwill and likely reach potential employers who will never see your website.

But they may well see a copy of your spreadsheet or guidelines or recipe that has been forwarded to them by someone else, and get in touch with you because they like what they've seen of your work. If they're really sensitive to the culture of the Web, they'll also recognize that out on the electronic frontier, pioneers lend a hand to one another — and since you've lent them a hand, they may be able to return the favor.

7.5 Make response easy

Your readers may well hop from page to page in your résumé. If they like what they see, getting in touch with you should be as easy as you can make it. This is really a design question inspired by the "you" attitude. For example, each page should have a link titled something like Email Me. Click on it, and an email form pops up, pre-addressed to you. Or each page could include your name and address plus telephone number(s) and email address. That way, readers always know how to reach you.

Ease of access, by the way, sends another nonverbal message: I'm thinking of your needs and making life as easy as I can for you.

Another thoughtful touch: In addition to your online résumé, whether scrolling or chunked, provide a version that employers can print out for themselves for easy reference. Keep it simple and short — not more than three pages and preferably one or two. Normally such a version would not contain elaborate formatting, links, or other Web-dependent effects: just words and white space, laid out for easy readability.

8

ADVOCACY AND MARKETING ON THE WEB

Information is telling people how many motels there are in Chesterton; advocacy is persuading people to visit Chesterton because it will meet their needs; and marketing is persuading people to make a reservation at one of those motels.

Many principles of advocacy and marketing in other media are the same online, but it's tempting to rely on web surfers' addiction to jolts to win them over. Resist the temptation. You wouldn't enjoy being conned or bullied into buying something, so don't expect it to work on your own website.

If your website's purpose is to promote a point of view or to sell an item or service, it's more likely to succeed if you respect your visitors. So keep in mind some basic principles of persuasion that can work while maintaining that respect.

1. Semantics and Register

Many words have complex connotations. That is, they don't just refer to a particular thing or action or idea; they convey some kind of emotional aura as well. A restaurant may be a "fast-food joint" or a "bistro" — both offer quick service, but a bistro sounds classier. "Good eats" promises something different from "an elegant dining experience."

Semantics is the study of such meanings, and semanticists like to distinguish between "purr words" and "snarl words" — words whose connotations are either positive (at least to the speaker or writer) or negative. Such words may refer to the same thing, but carry very different meanings: "Certified General Accountant" and "bean counter," for example, or "vintage automobile" and "beater," or "educator" and "pedant." In effect, purr words and snarl words convey our attitude toward whatever we're discussing.

As a persuasive webwriter, then, you should be aware of how your readers will respond to the words you choose. You should also consider the register to adopt in your text. Register involves choosing words that reflect your understanding of the social situation and how the people involved see one another.

When you write to a stranger, you address her as "Dear Ms. Robinson." That's the register of formal business writing, and Ms. Robinson accepts this term as a courtesy one stranger pays to another. Once you've become friends, you can write "Dear Helen," in a much less formal register. And what happens when you write "Dearest," or "Sweetest Helen." Suddenly you're in a much more intimate register, and you'd better hope she doesn't write back, "Dear Mr. Smith"!

Register doesn't just convey the proper manners for the occasion. It can also determine the content of your message. When the new President Obama addressed the nation after being sworn in, he didn't say: "Hi, folks." He said: "My fellow citizens." As a rule, the more people you're addressing at once, the more formal and abstract your message is likely to be. The fewer people you're addressing, the more informal and personal you can be.

What does that mean for you as a webwriter? Maybe thousands of people will visit your site; should you adopt an elevated "public" register, as if you were addressing a huge political rally? Or, since each reader arrives at your site as an individual, can you adopt an intimate personal register?

That depends to some extent on the nature of your site. If its purpose is to represent a "serious" organization — a bank, an environmental activist group, a political party's local branch — then the register should be serious also. Such organizations exist because of people's hopes and anxieties. No one wants to be even more anxious about the security of their savings or the direction their country is taking because of reading text with an inappropriate tone on an organization's website.

This is why bankers and politicians tend to dress conservatively, unless they're trying for a "plain folks" image. They also speak conservatively and would expect cautious, correct language on their organization's website.

If the organization's purpose is fun, then the register ought to convey that. The website for a company that makes squirt guns or that markets backpacks to young world travelers is obviously going to be relaxed and lighthearted. It can afford to use slang or incorrect English, or even to exclude some people by using in-group terms.

Whether serious or fun, your site is trying to assure your readers that you speak their language, and that they can, therefore, trust you. If your use of semantics and register makes them feel like outsiders, they will be skeptical of your claims.

2. Three Elements of Persuasion

When you're writing to persuade your readers, you may have varied goals. If you want to reinforce readers' existing beliefs and values (also known as preaching to the choir), you have an easy job. We're always eager to hear that we're right.

Changing your readers' beliefs is harder, and requires trust from your readers that you are concerned with their best interests.

Hardest of all is getting people to act, even when you've been telling them they're right.

Bear in mind the major elements of good webwriting: orientation, information, and action. If you make it easy for your readers to respond, they will get in the habit of acting.

Short, powerful chunks of text can trigger strong emotions and willingness to act. In some ways, the Web poses an ethical problem for the persuader: It's not suitable for careful, linear, logical argument, and it's excellent for jolt-rich slogans, captions, and unsupported assertions. Yet manipulating readers by appealing to their fears and insecurities is deeply disrespectful. If you're trying to persuade your readers, it should be on the basis of appeals to their intelligence and maturity.

With that in mind, let's look at three aspects of persuasion as they operate on the Web.

2.1 Logical argument

Logical argument involves stating a proposition of some kind, along with supporting reasons. The reasons themselves must be supportable. So you might predict that the US population in 2050 will reach 394 million, with 20 million being women aged 80 or more. You could cite the US Bureau of the Census as your support for this argument, and perhaps that would be enough authority for most people.

If you think it is not enough for your particular audience, you would also have to describe the Census Bureau's methodology in reaching its prediction. Assuming that the methodology used generally accepted statistical projections (accepted because they've been accurate in the past), you could safely assert that you've made a logical argument for your population forecast.

2.2 Appeal to authority

Some of us, thanks to personal experience and training, know more about some subjects than others. If I'm planning a trip to Cambodia, and you lived there for two years, I'll accept your advice and pass it along: "My friend who lived in Phnom Penh says … " And if I'm not a climatologist but I'm worried about human-caused global warming, I'll read what climatologists say, and why they say it. Then I'll come to my own conclusions.

What if some climatologists say human-caused global warming is real, and other say it's not? Then I'll have to look at their methods of research, and their logic, and decide accordingly.

2.3 Emotional appeal

By invoking ideas and images that stir our readers' feelings, we can gain interest that logical argument and appeal to authority may not achieve. In some cases, we may not even care about the logic in an argument until something has dragged us emotionally into a confrontation with the issue. Only then will some people seek the logical argument to back up their strong feelings.

Again, the online advocate should be careful to avoid exploiting readers' anxieties. Appeals to emotion should be positive (invoking love, trust, friendship, or noble qualities like courage and honesty), rather than appealing to fear, hatred, and contempt.

This doesn't mean a positive emotional appeal is automatically a good argument. Love and courage are admirable, but they may serve detestable causes.

Unless you support a position because of strong emotions you don't want to examine, you probably came to your position by learning particular facts. These facts, in the context of your particular values, caused you to adopt the position you're now advocating. You may, therefore, find that facts, not loaded language, can inspire similar emotions in your readers.

2.4 Credibility

Using your readers' language and registers they're comfortable with can strongly enhance your credibility. After all, you're showing that you share exformation with them.

But you also need to demonstrate some kind of shared interest between yourself and your readers, and convey sincerity through your tone and evident desire to help readers who visit your site. You should also have acceptable credentials — direct personal experience, specialized training, or at least a selection of respected and recognized authorities who can back up your assertions.

Relying on the "you" attitude can help your credibility by putting your arguments in terms of the reader's interest rather than your own. In its crudest form, this gives us the "crazy" retailer who's giving you a bargain that will probably bankrupt him or her. But if you can establish that you serve your own interests best by serving your reader's interests, you further enhance reader trust in you.

Some unscrupulous persuaders like to "stack the deck" by presenting only the information that makes them look good. A more effective way to establish credibility is to raise opposing arguments as serious objections — and then refute them. A frequently asked questions (FAQs) page — a page where such questions are cited and then answered — can also be an effective way to state your readers' reservations and show how you can demolish them.

3. Constructing Persuasive Webtext

Maybe you just want readers to accept your argument passively, but more likely you want them to act on it — to buy the product, vote for the candidate, protest the outrage. As we've seen, webtext doesn't lend itself to long, cumulative, reasoned argument, and it doesn't have the emotionally overwhelming impact of a wide-screen movie with stereo sound. Given its limits, the medium can still stir readers to respond to your message if you remember the principles of orientation, information, and action.

3.1 Orientation

Your readers want to know where they are when they arrive at your site, and they also want to know where they stand in relation to you. If they feel you're on their side, they'll welcome your message more easily. You can establish rapport with readers by using these techniques:

- **Show you understand your readers' concerns.** You can often do this by identifying something that your readers will recognize as a problem. The problem could be an oppressive government or the difficulty of saving money for a holiday.

- **Offer something that readers will agree with.** A generalization or striking slogan can make readers think they've found a kindred soul. It doesn't have to be a cliché, but it should state, as Alexander Pope observed, "what oft was thought, but ne'er so well expressed."

- **Ask for help.** Readers have the power to decide, to choose, to buy, to join, and you want readers to be aware of that power.

- **Suggest a benefit.** If your readers agree that a problem exists, offer a solution they will find beneficial: greater peace of mind, a clear conscience, a new experience.

3.2 Information

Your readers will want details of the facts backing up your argument. By providing further information, your argument becomes more legitimate and appealing to your readers. Try the following:

- Explain the benefit in some detail, using facts and figures if necessary.

- Surprise your reader with a new fact or perspective on a familiar subject; a reader with a new idea or understanding is open to persuasion. We trust people who are on our wavelength but ahead of us in understanding the issue.

- Discuss objections or drawbacks calmly, then rebut them and focus on positive arguments. Most of us have been fooled often enough to be suspicious of offers and arguments that are literally too good to be true, so readers will be suspicious even when they want to believe you.

3.3 Action

Make sure your argument ends with a strong call to action. The following tips can help encourage readers to take whatever action you would like them to take:

- **Show how action can solve the problem you've described.** You may give examples of earlier actions that got the desired results (Last year's campaign paid for clean water supplies for six villages) or unhappy results based on failure to act (Sixty-two children in the region died of cholera last year because of contaminated water).

- **Make the desired action clear and easy.** A complicated or time-consuming response will make your reader hesitate. (Just type in your name and email address. Simply click on the Yes or No button to register your opinion instantly! Test your understanding with this quick quiz.)

- **Stress the benefit of responding quickly.** Whether you're selling Alaska cruises or party memberships, delay can be fatal to your campaign. If appropriate, set a deadline: Email us by September 15 and get a free consultation ($250 value).

4. What's a Legitimate Appeal? What's Not?

You can legitimately appeal to —

- Recognized authorities — people or organizations generally accepted as expert and reliable in their field

- Scientific experiment and observation, producing results that others can duplicate

- Logical deduction or extrapolation from established facts

- Readers' emotions, but only when combined with other legitimate appeals

You're on shaky ground if you appeal to —

- Anecdotal evidence (My cousin was abducted by aliens)

- Celebrity (Scarlett Johansson supports Barack Obama!)

- Outside authorities trading on irrelevant expertise (Joe Doakes, a nuclear physicist, says UFOs exist)

You're out of bounds if you appeal to —

- Logical fallacies — mistakes in argument that sound logical but aren't (see Stephen's Guide to the Logical Fallacies Website at www.intrepidsoftware.com/fallacy/welcome.htm)

- Hasty generalizations (I lost a fortune in a Canadian casino; Canadians are a bunch of crooks)

- Wishful thinking (This stock is sure to go up)

- Readers' prejudices (Are you sick of the disaster in the public schools?)

- False authorities (The document *The Protocols of the Elders of Zion* proves the Jews want to take over the world — this argument is still made by anti-Semites, though the *Protocols* were long ago proven to be a forgery of the Tsarist secret police who plagiarized them from a French satire on Napoleon III published in the 1860s)

5. Notes on Propaganda

When you write advocacy text, you're a propagandist, but that's not always a bad thing. Propaganda tries to influence large numbers of people, using the mass media as its chief vehicles: print, film, TV, and radio. Millions of websites are now propaganda vehicles also. Like any any other form of persuasion, a website appeals to both reason and emotion. However, it tends to rely more heavily on emotional appeals since it must reach such a large and varied audience.

As an honest advocate, you should be aware of what propaganda can and can't do, and what it should and should not do. This means understanding the types of propaganda, the attitudes that it relies on, and the ways that propaganda techniques may be abused.

6. Major Types of Propaganda

- **Social**: Develops or strengthens attitudes and beliefs over the long term, especially in news broadcasts, entertainment, sports. Example: a string of government scandals that make the ruling party look corrupt and incompetent. Many political blogs promote social propaganda.

- **Shock**: Mobilizes audience over a short time, using attitudes developed by social propaganda. Examples: TV election ads attacking government corruption and incompetence; US government warnings about Iraqi weapons of mass destruction in 2002-03. The "shock" is not to scandalize or outrage, but to motivate the audience to act.

- **Black**: The other side's propaganda or beliefs, or something supposedly expressing the other side's views. Example: In the early days of the Iraq War, the propaganda efforts of the Saddam regime were so obviously wrong that they became excellent propaganda for the US-led coalition.

- **Silent**: Suppressing or ignoring inconvenient or damaging information. Example: No broadcasting of gory videos from war zones. Exposure of silent propaganda may result in both social-propaganda and shock-propaganda campaigns: "Here is what your evil government is really doing!"

7. Propaganda myths

In propaganda, a myth is an assertion about reality that may or may not be true, but which many of us strongly believe. Myths are often unprovable, outside the realm of verifiable fact, but millions of people have killed, tortured, and persecuted one another to uphold such unprovable beliefs. Here are some typical myths that, true or not, have inspired much modern propaganda:

- **Progress**: Everything's getting better; tomorrow will be better than today; yesterday was awful. Our supporters are advanced and progressive; our enemies are dinosaurs and cave men.

- **The Last Judgment**: We'll pay for our crimes/errors some day. So we should stop oppressing people, exploiting women, damaging the environment, running up the deficit.

- **Racial Superiority**: Some races are smarter, nicer, sexier, more athletic, more law-abiding, or more criminal than others.

- **The Subhuman Enemy:** Our enemies are bestial and vicious and deserve no better treatment than animals. So cops are pigs, and the anti-war French are "surrender monkeys."

- **The Scapegoat:** Our problems are all due to the corporations, or the unions, or the immigrants. So we don't have to examine our own failings.

- **National Superiority/Inferiority**: Canadians are just like the Americans, only nicer. Swedes can't play rock'em sock'em hockey.

- **The Real Man:** A real man enlists for combat, wears the pants in his family, and doesn't eat quiche or write poems.

- **The Real Woman:** A real woman is attractive, fertile, enjoys the fine arts, and sacrifices herself for her husband and children.

- **The Conspiracy:** The CIA/Jewish bankers/World Trade Organization are causing all the trouble in the world.

- **The Underdog:** Whoever is smaller or weaker in a dispute is probably in the right.

- **The Martyr:** Our leader/companion vindicated our cause by dying for it.

- **The Great Leader:** Our leader personally embodies all our national/cultural/racial virtues.

8. Basic Propaganda Devices

Used properly, these devices can sometimes form part of rational debate. Most people who use them, however, only want to trigger strong emotions — not logical thought — in the target audience.

- **Name Calling**: "You dirty neocon/socialist/racist/sexist!"

- **Glittering Generalities**: "Liberty, equality, fraternity." "Peace, order, and good government." "Free trade." "Fair trade." Emotional but abstract words that make good slogans but poor policy.

- **Transfer**: Swastika, stars and stripes, maple leaf — powerful graphic symbols associated with something the propagandist wants people to support or oppose. Flag-burning, and burning in effigy, exploit the transfer device by symbolically destroying the enemy.

- **Testimonial**: Support for an idea based on authority ("Dr. Smith agrees"), celebrity ("Celine Dion agrees"), plain folks ("Bruce Smith agrees").

- **Card Stacking**: One-sided argument: "We have 85 percent full employment!" Closely related to silent propaganda.

- **Bandwagon**: Many supporters make an idea valid; few supporters make an idea invalid. "A growing number of concerned Canadians/A small but vocal gang of troublemakers ... "

- **Identity Threat**: "Our opponents are a menace to our nation/society/class/group/sexual orientation." One of the most powerful propaganda devices, used in election campaigns (which are shock propaganda) and in much social propaganda (everything from comic strips to news reports).

- **Triumph**: "We've done a great job, so re-elect us."

- **Outrage**: "They've done an awful job, so throw the bums out."

Paradoxes of Propaganda

- Much propaganda is personally and socially constructive. It encourages us to drive safely, treat others kindly, and obey the law.

- Propaganda works best on the converted. They always want more confirmation that they're right.

- Propaganda works best on educated people. Illiterate peasants don't know or care about the world beyond their village; university graduates think they can change the world.

- Truth is the best propaganda; next best is the half-truth; silence is usually preferable to an outright lie. If they catch you lying, like "Comical Ali" in the Iraq War, or the Chinese government in the SARS outbreak, they stop believing you.

- Enemy propaganda can be excellent propaganda for one's own side. (How can those idiots believe such claptrap!)

- Straight news or entertainment can conceal propaganda, especially social propaganda trying to confirm or change social attitudes. ("Tonight's news confirms all your prejudices about your provincial government, cruel military tyrants, and suffering people in the Third World.")

- Propaganda that seems to argue against its own self-interest is more credible. ("We teachers are overpaid. You should cut our salaries or demand more work from us.")

- When propaganda is really good, it can make people act against their own beliefs. ("I don't agree with either candidate, but I'll hold my nose and vote for the lesser of two evils.")

9. Analyzing Advocacy Websites

Countless websites and blogs argue for or against something. If you are writing for such a site, it can be helpful to review and critique a range of advocacy sites. But this can be challenging.

If you visit a site that supports the same things you do, it's easy to admire and imitate it. However, you don't want to preach to the proverbial choir — you want to make converts and win new supporters.

So look at both the competition and the opposition, and remember the "you" attitude. Put yourself in the shoes of the people who may visit such sites. Are they looking for reassurance, or for a whole new point of view? Are they looking for a way to solve a problem, or just trying to inform themselves?

My blog Writing for the Web (http://crofsblogs.typepad.com) has an online appendix to this book. In it you'll find links to a wide range of advocacy sites, from political parties to humanitarian nongovernmental organizations to religious groups. Assess such sites in the light of the kinds of appeals they make, and the kinds of propaganda myths they employ. How effective do they appear to be? Do they have a lot of traffic — and can you trust their public traffic statistics? Do visitors post many comments, and do those comments agree or disagree with the site's position? Do such comments reflect the kinds of people you would like to attract to your site?

Propaganda has a bad reputation for a good reason: Most propagandists understand their audiences, but have no respect for them. Their propaganda relies on the instrumental model. It wants to manipulate the audience into obeying the command "Do what I say!"

If you are more interested in launching a conversation with your audience, raising issues, and expecting to learn something from them, then the interactive communication model of the Web can serve you well. But not all who write advocacy on the Web have understood that.

9

FREQUENTLY ASKED QUESTIONS

The Web is already home to many flourishing genres, from muck-raking journalism to erotica to avant-garde fiction. Each of these genres probably deserves a book of its own, and will doubtless get it before long. The theory of such forms of webwriting will emerge from actual practice as thousands of writers experiment to see what works and what doesn't, right on the Web itself.

While looking forward to the appearance of such books, let's try to deal with some basic questions and point interested readers to the ongoing discussions that are attempting to answer them.

1. Can I Make Money as a Freelance Writer on the Web?

Some people can make money freelancing on the Web, and many are trying. In some cases, freelancers are simply using the Web as a faster way to pitch story ideas to editors of print-based periodicals.

In the mid-1990s, this often worked well because email was still a relative novelty and editors paid more attention to electronic queries. Since then, the flood of queries has caused many editors to ignore electronic queries on principle.

However, the websites that pay freelancers are usually the websites of newspapers and magazines that are fighting to stay alive. Print periodicals around the world are failing at a disturbing rate. The journalists they've laid off are launching their own blogs, trying to attract enough visitors to interest online advertisers. So don't quit your day job.

A good source for current (if depressing) news about online journalism is Poynter Online (www.poynter.org).

2. Can I Teach Webwriting?

Yes, you can teach webwriting. And as online sources become the preferred choice of billions of information seekers, competent webwriters should be in great demand.

You can't do it all yourself. Someone in your company or school has to be able to write web content besides you. So if you're the most experienced webwriter around, chances are you'll end up teaching your colleagues or students how to write for the Web.

You can teach webwriting successfully — especially if you set up your course or workshop so that your students really teach themselves. The principles that make a good website are also the principles that make a good course.

Start with the key question: Who's your audience? How narrowly can you define it? Do you want to reach nuclear physicists, cancer patients, hiphop fans?

And who, therefore, are your students? Are they colleagues in your company, or students just passing through your classroom? Why do they want to learn webwriting — to make themselves more employable in future, or to hang on to a job right now? Can they choose the kind of website they're creating, or must they accept an existing site as their workspace?

The answers to those questions will help determine both your course content and the style and tone in which you express it. You'll have to take your students' strengths and weaknesses as your starting point.

Any good website does the same thing: its purpose is to serve the user, not to flatter the creator. If your students don't know technical terms, then you'll have to avoid them (or define them clearly when you must use them). If they know XML but can't spell "extensible," then you'll have to spend time on correct spelling.

Coming out of a print-oriented business or school culture, your students will want to write long — but you know hypertext often works best in short, stand-alone chunks of 100 words or less. Students know when they're dealing with a good or bad site, but they may have trouble explaining why. And they may forget that this is an interactive medium that succeeds only when the user responds to the information on the site.

Here are six techniques to help your students teach themselves webwriting:

1. Tell your students to write a 500-word essay. After you've returned it with your comments and corrections, announce their second assignment: To cut the first essay by 50 percent or more ... and still have it hang together and make sense.

   Students are used to padding their essays with BS, but now the prize will go to the leanest, cleanest prose they can bring out of the first essay. You'll be amazed at how quickly and brutally they can cut their own work, and yours. (By the way, the first draft of this section was 1100 words long; it's now 821 words.)

2. Ask them to cut again until they get below that 100-word maximum for a chunk. They can't? Can they break the text into two chunks?

3. Further editing assignments, especially adapting long print text to the Web, will hone their skills and train them to find natural breaks between passages that can stand alone on the Web if need be.

4. Ask your students to write website reviews. Let them use their own standards, or apply those of some usability wizard like Jakob Nielsen. By writing about those sites, your students will have to articulate their opinions, not just say: "This sucks, that doesn't."

5. Ask for detailed proposals for their own sites: purpose, intended audience, content ... even the hours they estimate it will take them to write their web content. Then they can rough out a site map or outline, without having to improvise or hope for sudden inspiration.

6. Put students' draft webtext up on a chalkboard or overhead transparency so everyone can see it — and rip it apart. Is it short? Usable? Understandable? Does it invite response?

No doubt you'll want to do much more, but these assignments and activities have been the core of my own webwriting courses, and they've worked.

What's more, they've worked in a regular classroom, not in a computer lab. Put students in front of networked computers, and they're all over the planet before you can give them the first URL you want them to find. Use a single computer and a projector in a darkened classroom, and they fall asleep. If they're spending the rest of their day staring at a monitor, they'll be grateful not to have to do so in your class.

Plan on something else important: Your students won't just teach themselves. They'll teach you a lot about this medium and the way words work in it. The interactivity isn't just on the site — it'll happen in your class as well. And you'll go on learning something new every time you teach how to write for the Web.

3. Can I Create My Own E-zine?

Sure, you can create your own e-zine. The line is blurring between the original e-zines such as *Salon*, and today's multiple-author blogs. Both genres are trying to attract large audiences and thereby attract advertising.

Some online magazines and blogs solicit advertisers directly, charging a small sum for each reader who clicks through the ad to the advertiser's own site. Others make a deal with Google or other agencies, which provide topic-related ads. But be careful. If you're running a site about psoriasis or lung cancer, you may find yourself displaying ads for quack remedies.

And you may have to choose your words carefully even if your site has no medical aspects: Tell the world you're depressed today, and you could be advertising online antidepressants!

The question is whether your e-zine will attract enough readers to interest advertisers. If it does, advertising will help pay the costs of the e-zine and maybe even pay you something. If it doesn't, your e-zine will just be a hobby.

As with any other form of self-publishing, you should consider whether you're a writer, a businessperson, or both. If you're primarily a writer, looking after the business end of running an e-zine will be time taken away from what you really enjoy doing. If you enjoy both writing and business, an e-zine could be an ideal way to combine your interests.

4. Can I Write Hypertext Fiction for the Web?

Yes, you can write hypertext fiction for the Web, but it's a highly demanding form in which no one has more than a few years' experience. If you are interested in exploring this genre, the best place to start is probably the Eastgate Systems home page: www.eastgate.com.

Eastgate has been actively promoting hypertext fiction since the late 1980s, and has published pioneering work in the field. Its site also supplies links to many other hypertext-fiction resources on the Web.

Other hypertext-fiction sites tend to be short-lived. For some general information, and a few links, see the Wikipedia entry: (http://en.wikipedia.org/wiki/Hypertext_fiction).

5. Can I Copyright My Webwriting?

Yes, you can copyright your webwriting but the issues surrounding intellectual property are complex and rapidly changing.

For example, some writers have found that when they sell an article to a print magazine or newspaper, they've also unwittingly given away the electronic rights in perpetuity. The publishers can put the articles up on their periodicals' websites and use them to attract other readers, who in turn attract advertisers, who pay the publishers. But the publishers don't have to split that income with the writers, because the publishers hold the rights to the articles.

Many writers' organizations are fighting this practice, and freelancers are trying to get their publishers to state in advance exactly what rights they're buying. It will doubtless remain a vexing problem for years to come, especially in a medium where copying is so easy and copyright enforcement so difficult.

Meanwhile, you may find yourself violating someone else's copyright — knowingly or otherwise — by pasting parts of some web-published document into your own work. It's always a good idea to get permission from the copyright holder before you use even a graphic from someone else's site. You may find that the holder of the copyright will grant permission to copy in return for a link on your site to the original item.

The following websites should give you a general sense of how copyright affects you and your work:

- Creative Commons: http://creativecommons.org

- Electronic Frontier Foundation (an important site for many other resources as well): www.eff.org/pub/Intellectual_ property

- Intellectual Property on the Net: www.cpsr.org/program/nii/IP.html

- Digital Future Coalition: www.dfc.org

- International Federation of Library Associations: Copyright and Intellectual Property: www.ifla.org/II/copyright.htm

- World Intellectual Property Organization: www.wipo.int

- US Copyright Office: http://lcweb.loc.gov/copyright

- American Society of Journalists and Authors: The Basics About Copyright Registration: www.asja.org

6. How Do I Cite Web Sources in Scholarly Writing?

The Web is becoming an indispensable research tool (and equally indispensable for plagiarists), but it's happened so fast that authorities are still developing standard forms of citation. Generally accepted types of citations follow this basic format:

Author. "Article Title." Periodical/Book Title. Date given on web page. Date accessed by reader. URL.

The author's name appears last name first (if the item has more than one author, subsequent authors appear with first name first). The title of the article appears in quotation marks, with a period inside the close quotation. The name of the periodical or book appears with the main words capitalized and the whole title italicized or underlined. The date of the web page is given as well as the date you accessed it, since of course the page may well have changed since you did so.

For example:

Kilian, Crawford. "The Visions of Ji Won Park." The Tyee. May 29, 2006. Accessed February 7, 2009. http://thetyee.ca/Photo/2006/05/29/JiWon

For more detailed guidelines, consult these online resources:

- Research and Documentation Online: http://dianahacker.com/resdoc

- Columbia Guide to Online Style: www.columbia.edu/cu/cup/cgos/idx_basic.html

- Electronic Citation Guides (University of Texas at El Paso Library): http://libraryweb.utep.edu/db/citing.cfm

- Journalism Resource: Guide to Citation Style Guides: http://bailiwick.lib.uiowa.edu/journalism/cite.html

7. Can a Website Enhance a Book on Paper?

Yes, a website can enhance a printed book. More and more textbooks offer websites as a way to update and expand their print content. Other kinds of books are doing the same. The Twilight novels by Stephenie Meyer have an official website (www.stepheniemeyer.com) as well as countless fan sites.

In nonfiction, websites enable content to stay current without producing a whole new print edition. In 2008 I published a new edition of my book *Go Do Some Great Thing*, which has its own site: http://crofsblogs.typepad.com/pioneers, which began as a workspace for the book and is now a promotional and update site.

In fiction (and nonfiction as well, no doubt), websites give readers an opportunity to respond directly to the author and publisher. This is already happening even when authors and publishers don't yet have their own sites: On the Amazon.com bookselling site, for example, visitors can post their own reviews of books they've read, and authors can respond — authors can even review their own books if they like!

Many publishers are already posting excerpts from print books on the web as a way to stir up interest in the book. This follows a practice of some paperback publishing houses, which may include an excerpt from a forthcoming book in the back of another novel — like the Coming Attractions at a movie. Some publishers are even putting whole manuscripts online. Readers can either read the whole book onscreen (often paying to do so), or pay for a custom-printed copy. Authors themselves are divided on the value of such schemes.

8. How Can I Attract Visitors to My Site?

Attracting visitors to your site can be a problem. Designers used to bury dozens of "invisible" keywords at the top of a home page, to attract search engines. A porn site might bury "sex" and related words, repeated hundreds of times, to bring themselves to the top of the hit list.

Search engines today are smarter than they used to be. Today, such buried keywords will get the site kicked to the bottom of the list.

You can attract traffic if you title your site with a word or phrase your audience is like to use in looking for you. That's why I called my flu blog "H5N1: News and resources about avian flu." Inevitably, I use H5N1 and avian flu and bird flu in most of my posts.

Even so, I was surprised to find that within a few months, Google put my site on the first page of its search results for "H5N1"; in January 2009, an advanced Google search for that term turned up 6 million hits, and my blog was sixth from the top.

For more detailed advice on attracting traffic, visit these sites:

- SuccessWorks: www.searchenginewriting.com

- SEO Chat: www.seochat.com

- Search Engine Optimization Journal:
  www.searchengineoptimizationjournal.com

- Webworx Factory:
  http://webworxfactory.com/category/search-engine-optimization

9. How Can Writers and Graphic Designers Work Together?

I'll let graphic designer Chris Zawada answer this one:

The best way writers can work with designers is essentially just that ... working together. Most of the time the designer and writer will work in separate bubble: the writer will write a block of text which he or she feels works best for the client's need ... and separately the designer will design and drop in the amount of "lorem ipsum" text that he or she feels works best esthetically with the design.

Unfortunately, more often than not the final copy will be either too long or too short for the space the designer allotted. When the two parties can work together and bounce ideas off each other, and keep each other up to speed with design and copy, this problem can easily be averted.

APPENDIX

Exercise Key

Exercise 4: Converting Prose to Bullets

The key conventions of modern science fiction:

- Isolated society (island, lost valley, planet)

- Morally significant language (Orwell's Newspeak)

- Important documents (Book of Bokonon in Vonnegut's *Cat's Cradle*)

- Ideological attitude toward sex (Huxley's *Brave New World*)

- An inquisitive outsider (Genly Ai in Le Guin's *The Left Hand of Darkness*)

Here are active-voice versions of the passive-voice sentences. Other versions could be equally acceptable.

1. Some researchers argue that the US Air Force retrieved alien bodies from a crashed spacecraft near Roswell, New Mexico, in 1947.

2. Critics hailed Miles Davis's Sketches of Spain as one of his finest works.

3. Researchers at Xerox originally developed the graphical user interface.

4. A local physician stopped a 19th-century outbreak of cholera in London by removing the handle from a neighborhood water pump.

5. We carefully chose these graphics to illustrate each step of the process.

Exercise 7: Using Anglo-Saxon Vocabulary

1. altercation: angry dispute

2. antagonist: adversary, opponent

3. capitulate: give up, surrender

4. celestial: pertaining to the sky or heavens

5. demotic: common, popular

6. epitome: typical (or extreme) example; concise summary

7. fiduciary: acting as trustee or guardian; held in trust

8. gravamen: most serious part of an accusation; essential part or gist

9. impediment: obstacle, handicap

10. litigious: quarrelsome; quick to go to court

AFTERWORD

In a book about interactive writing, no one has the last word — least of all the author. Whether you've read this book line by line, or hopped around in it as if it were hypertext, you've been engaged in some kind of dialogue with it. Maybe you scribbled in the margins, or threw the book across the room. Maybe you changed your website, or perhaps you left it exactly as it was to show how unimpressed you are by my arguments.

But the Web is designed for dialogue as print is not. If you have questions, comments, objections, or worries about what you've read here, by all means let me know. You can reach me at:

crof@shaw.ca

And you can also reach me through my blogs:

Writing for the Web: http://crofsblogs.typepad.com

Writing Fiction: http://crofsblogs.typepad.com/fiction

Ask the English Teacher: http://crofsblogs.typepad.com/english

H5N1: http://crofsblogs.typepad.com/h5n1

OTHER TITLES OF INTEREST FROM SELF-COUNSEL PRESS!

Start & Run a Real Home-Based Business
Dan Furman
ISBN: 978-1-55180-866-6
$20.95 US/$23.95 CDN

If you're looking for yet another useless, "fluff-filled" book on home-based businesses, then this book isn't for you. Instead, this book is for real people who want to run a real business, and the updated second edition contains even more tips for entrepreneurs.

Learn how to:

- Make good money working from home
- Profit from skills you already have
- Stop dreaming — start doing

Financial Management 101
Angie Mohr, CA, CMA
ISBN: 978-1-55180-805-5
$16.95 US/$18.95 CDN

Angie Mohr's easy-to-understand approach to small-business planning and management ensures that the money coming in is always greater than the money going out!

- Analyze financial data to stay in touch with the heart of your business
- Measure your business success and pinpoint new opportunities
- Understand your business from the inside out

Business Writing Basics
Jane Watson
978-1-55180-769-0
$12.95 USD/$14.95 CAD

Make a good impression on clients, colleagues, and even your employer with effective business writing skills. While a poorly written letter can embarrass an organization, a professionally penned document will enhance the image of both the company and the writer.

Learn how you can —

- Adopt a "you" attitude when writing for the web
- Plan and write business cases and reports
- Plan and write reports
- Replace clichés and other antiquated phrases
- Use verbs that create powerful messages
- Avoid writer's block

Writing Science Fiction and Fantasy
Crawford Kilian
ISBN: 978-1-55180-785-0
$16.95 US/$21.95 CDN

Are you struggling to get started on your science fiction or fantasy novel? Stuck at chapter two or need a fresh approach? Find new direction and inspiration with this unique guide to creating original and convincing stories. Written by a successful author of more than ten science fiction and fantasy novels, *Writing Science Fiction and Fantasy* takes an in-depth look at these two best-selling genres. Learn about:

- Constructing a scene
- Showing versus telling
- Avoiding clichés
- Developing good writing and research habits
- Creating plausible fantasy worlds
- Using symbolism and imagery effectively

Writing Romance

Vanessa Grant
ISBN: 978-1-55180-739-3
$19.95 US/$24.95 CDN

Romance novels represent one of the most lucrative genres in book publishing — making up over half of all mass market fiction sold in North America and generating more than $1.2 billion a year. This book will show you everything you need to know to successfully break into the romance writing market, from planning and plotting your story to editing and selling your manuscript.

- Develop characters your readers will care about
- Write sensual and romantic scenes
- Set up a suspenseful story
- Research your plot details
- Use your computer to write efficiently
- Work with an agent
- Find a publisher
- Sell your book

Study Smarter, Not Harder

Kevin Paul
ISBN: 978-1-55180-741-6
$17.95 USD/$22.95 CAD

At work or at school, requirements rise higher and higher as competition grows fiercer. We are constantly challenged by having to acquire new skills and ideas as those we've learned become obsolete.

By mastering the seven basic elements of complete study skills included in this book, you can tap into your hidden potential for maximum performance and increased learning power.

- Use the genius inside you
- Expand your memory capacity 100 times
- Energize your brain

Low-Budget Online Marketing for Small Business
Holly Berkley
ISBN: 978-1-55180-634-1
$14.95 USD/$19.95 CAD

Large companies have huge budgets for marketing their products and services online. What's the difference between a $100,000 marketing campaign and a $1,000 campaign? Surprisingly, not much. This book teaches small-business operators how to achieve big-business marketing success on a small-business budget!

Low-Budget Online Marketing for Small Business takes you behind the scenes of successful marketing campaigns. This book will show you how to cut costs so that you can adapt the same successful marketing strategies that big companies use.

Marketing in the New Media
Holly Berkley
ISBN: 978-1-55180-872-7
$18.95 USD/ $19.95 CAD

Many small-business owners and marketing professionals are entering into new, unfamiliar territory, and the thought of stepping out of their comfort zones and diving into the fast-moving world of new media is intimidating. By giving case studies of companies that combined television, radio, and/or print with new media marketing, and showing exactly how people are using the latest technologies, Berkley explains how to analyze your online customer behaviors on a deeper level. Learn how to:

- unlock the secrets of successful website design
- break into social network sites
- get high rankings in today's top search engines
- form a personal relationship with your customers with e-newsletters
- sponsor podcasts, video files, and video games
- explore the world of mobile marketing (via text messages on cell phones)